READ WELL®

Assessment Manual

Placement, Diagnosis, and Prescription

Research Snapshot

REGULAR ASSESSMENT IS THE KEY TO INDIVIDUALLY APPROPRIATE INSTRUCTION

Use the *Read Well* assessment system with fidelity.

Following a review of the research on normal reading development, reading instruction, and factors related to reading failure, the National Research Council (1998) recommended ongoing assessment of word recognition and fluency as a critical component of excellent reading instruction.

"Because the ability to obtain meaning from print depends so strongly on the development of word recognition accuracy and reading fluency, both the latter should be regularly assessed in the classroom, permitting timely and effective instructional response when difficulty or delay is apparent" (Snow, Burns, & Griffin, 1998, p. 7).

Critical Foundations in Primary Reading

Marilyn Sprick, Ann Watanabe, Karen Akiyama-Paik, and Shelley V. Jones

Copyright 2009 Sopris West Educational Services. All rights reserved.

ISBN 13-digit: 978-1-60218-522-7
ISBN 10-digit: 1-60218-522-0

13 12 11 10 09 08   2 3 4 5 6 7

166828

Sopris West®
EDUCATIONAL SERVICES

A Cambium Learning® Company

BOSTON, MA · LONGMONT, CO

Table of Contents

Table of Contents *(continued)*

Table of Contents (continued)

Introduction

Placement

Each child enters the next grade level with his or her own unique literacy histories and abilities. To ensure success and adequate progress in reading, it is crucial to take great care in placing each child in an appropriate instructional group.

During the first week of school, use the *Read Well* Placement System to place children into appropriate reading groups. Keep in mind that these groups are flexible. Students will move in and out of groups based on their performance on assessments throughout the program.

Beginning Small Group Instruction

To provide each child with optimal instructional time, small group instruction should begin by the second or third week of school. Daily instruction focuses on the five critical areas of early reading instruction identified by the National Reading Panel (2000): phonemic awareness, phonics, fluency, vocabulary, and comprehension. Instruction is systematic, explicit, rich in content, and mastery based.

Cycle of Assessment and Instruction

Once children are in small groups, regular end-of-unit Oral Reading Fluency Assessments provide ongoing progress monitoring. Prescriptive teaching follows diagnosis with lesson planning and instruction tailored to the developmental needs of each group and every child. Guidelines for acceleration, early intervention, and group reviews help maximize the progress of each child. Beginning in Unit 5, optional Written Assessments are also available. These informal assessments can also be used as an additional Comprehension and Skill Activity.

Every Child Deserves
to *Read Well*®

SECTION 1

Placement

This section explains how to use the Placement System to group students for success.

Placement Overview

Recognizing that schools often have their own battery of extensive required assessments, the *Fluency Foundations* and *Read Well 2* Placement System is a series of in-program Oral Reading Fluency Assessments. These assessments are quick to administer, but accurate for preliminary placement in *Fluency Foundations* or *Read Well 2*.

If students do not pass the requirements for entry into *Fluency Foundations* or *Read Well 2*, they are assessed for placement in *Read Well 1*, using the *Read Well 1* Placement Inventory.

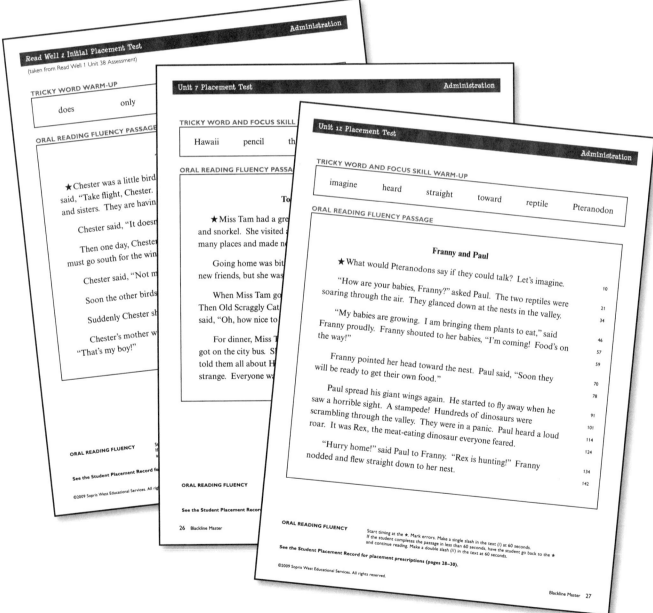

Read Well 2 Initial Placement Test
(taken from Read Well 1 Unit 38 Assessment)

Administration

TRICKY WORD WARM-UP

does   only

ORAL READING FLUENCY PASSAGE

★Chester was a little bird
said, "Take flight, Chester.
and sisters. They are havin

Chester said, "It doesn

Then one day, Chester
must go south for the win

Chester said, "Not m

Soon the other birds

Suddenly Chester sh

Chester's mother w
"That's my boy!"

ORAL READING FLUENCY

See the Student Placement Record fo

©2009 Sopris West Educational Services. All rig

Unit 7 Placement Test

Administration

TRICKY WORD AND FOCUS SKILL

Hawaii   pencil   th

ORAL READING FLUENCY PASSA

To

★Miss Tam had a gre
and snorkel. She visited
many places and made n

Going home was bit
new friends, but she was

When Miss Tam go
Then Old Scraggly Cat
said, "Oh, how nice to

For dinner, Miss T
got on the city bus. S
told them all about H
strange. Everyone w

ORAL READING FLUENCY

See the Student Placement Recor

26 Blackline Master

Unit 12 Placement Test

Administration

TRICKY WORD AND FOCUS SKILL WARM-UP

imagine   heard   straight   toward   reptile   Pteranodon

ORAL READING FLUENCY PASSAGE

Franny and Paul

★What would Pteranodons say if they could talk? Let's imagine.

"How are your babies, Franny?" asked Paul. The two reptiles were
soaring through the air. They glanced down at the nests in the valley.

"My babies are growing. I am bringing them plants to eat," said
Franny proudly. Franny shouted to her babies, "I'm coming! Food's on
the way!"

Franny pointed her head toward the nest. Paul said, "Soon they
will be ready to get their own food."

Paul spread his giant wings again. He started to fly away when he
saw a horrible sight. A stampede! Hundreds of dinosaurs were
scrambling through the valley. They were in a panic. Paul heard a loud
roar. It was Rex, the meat-eating dinosaur everyone feared.

"Hurry home!" said Paul to Franny. "Rex is hunting!" Franny
nodded and flew straight down to her nest.

10
21
34
46
57
59
70
78
91
101
114
124
134
142

ORAL READING FLUENCY

Start timing at the ★. Mark errors. Make a single slash in the text (/) at 60 seconds.
If the student completes the passage in less than 60 seconds, have the student go back to the ★
and continue reading. Make a double slash (//) in the text at 60 seconds.

See the Student Placement Record for placement prescriptions (pages 28–30).

©2009 Sopris West Educational Services. All rights reserved.

Blackline Master 27

General Placement and Program Information

Placement is determined by the results of *Read Well* placement testing. Students can place into *Read Well* programs at various entry points.

2ND GRADE ENTRY		PROGRAM INFORMATION
Read Well 1 Units 1, 4, 6, 10, 16, 21, 24, 30	• Intervention • Intensive Intervention	*Read Well 1* provides systematic and explicit instruction in first grade reading skills. Units can be adjusted to meet the needs of all students. If mastery is acquired quickly, students can move through the program rapidly.
Fluency Foundations Unit A	Core (foundation building)	*Fluency Foundations* provides a quick review of *Read Well 1* skills for low-average readers who will benefit from instruction and practice to build fluency. This systematic review accelerates the progress of low-average readers.
Read Well 2 Units 1, 8, 13	Core	*Read Well 2* provides a rich second grade curriculum. Students who place in *Read Well 2* will complete the year above grade level.

3RD GRADE ENTRY		PROGRAM INFORMATION
Read Well 1 Units 1, 4, 6, 10, 16, 21, 24, 30	Intensive Intervention	*Read Well 1* provides systematic and explicit instruction in first grade reading skills. Units can be adjusted to meet the needs of all students. If mastery is acquired quickly, students can move through the program rapidly.
Fluency Foundations Unit A	Intervention	*Fluency Foundations* provides a quick review of *Read Well 1* skills for students reading below grade level. *Fluency Foundations* is appropriate for third grade students who have acquired but not mastered first grade skills.
Read Well 1 Plus or	Intervention	*Read Well 1 Plus* provides instruction in second grade skills. Students who complete *Read Well 1 Plus* read at a high second to beginning third grade level.
Read Well 2 Units 1–12 then		*Read Well 2* Units 1–12 provide instruction in phonics skills that parallel *Read Well 1 Plus*. *Read Well 2* includes the introduction of more vocabulary words and a broader array of writing and comprehension activities. The broader units in *Read Well 2* Units 1–12 may require more instructional time to reach the same level of reading fluency as the equivalent units in *Read Well 1 Plus*.
Read Well 2 Unit 13–25		Third grade students who complete *Read Well 2* Unit 25 will be at or above a 3.5 grade level equivalency.

Students can enter *Read Well 2* Unit 13 after successfully completing either *Read Well 1 Plus* or *Read Well 2* Units 1–12.

Managing the Placement System

What to Administer

The Placement System includes end-of-unit Oral Reading Fluency Assessments from *Read Well 1* Unit 38—the *Read Well 2* Initial Placement Test—*Read Well 2* Unit 7, and *Read Well 2* Unit 12. Students who do not place into *Fluency Foundations* or *Read Well 2* should be assessed for placement into *Read Well 1* for intervention. (See *Read Well 1 Assessment Manual*.)

When to Administer

The placement tests should be administered to all second grade students and remedial third grade students during the first week of school. A quick start is strongly recommended because the loss of a week or two of instruction can make the difference in whether or not high-risk students achieve grade level. *Read Well 2* begins with a Start-Up Unit that provides four or six days of whole class instruction. This gives teachers and assistants time to assess students for placement into small groups without compromising precious instructional time.

Who Administers

Each school varies in its opening routines and resources. Consider the following options for completing the placement testing:

- Have a trained assessment team administer the placement tests to individual students while the teacher continues teaching. Team members could include counselors, paraprofessionals, resource teachers, part-time teachers, and other support staff.

- Have pairs of teachers team teach part of the day. While one teacher assesses his or her class, the other teacher instructs both classes. Then teachers switch.

- If assistance or teaming is not available, classroom teachers can assess a few students each day—completing testing in the first two weeks of school. Placement tests can be administered to individual students while others complete the Start-Up Unit's independent work.

Materials Preparation

1. ***Read Well 2* Student Placement Record:** Make one copy per student of the Student Placement Record (page 28). This form is used to record and score students' responses. Keep the Student Placement Record in each student's file or portfolio as a pretest measure.

2. ***Read Well 2* Units 7 and 12 Student Assessment Records:** For each person who will administer the placement tests, make additional copies of the *Read Well 2* Unit 7 and Unit 12 Student Placement Records (pages 29 and 30). These assessments will be used only with children who score 100 or more words correct per minute (WCPM). (Refer to the Administration and Placement Schedule on page 12.)

3. ***Read Well 1* Assessment Manual:** For students who score 54 or fewer WCPM, administer the *Read Well 1* Placement Inventory, which can be found in the *Read Well 1 Assessment Manual*. Keep the *Read Well 1* Student Placement Record in the student's file or portfolio. If *Read Well 1* is not available, you will need to find a comparable intervention program for any student scoring 54 or fewer WCPM.

4. **Placement Test and System Administration Page:** For each test administrator, make copies of the *Read Well 2* Initial Placement Test as well as the Unit 7 and Unit 12 Placement Tests found on pages 25–27 in this guide. You may wish to laminate the pages for each tester or place the pages in plastic sheet protectors.

5. **Stopwatches:** Obtain stopwatches for each tester. The assessments include timings to measure students' reading fluency.

6. **Clipboards and Pencils:** Place the Student Placement Records on clipboards for each person administering the Placement System. Have pencils for each administrator.

7. **Test Administration Area:** Set up a quiet place to administer the Placement System. Students should be seated at a table.

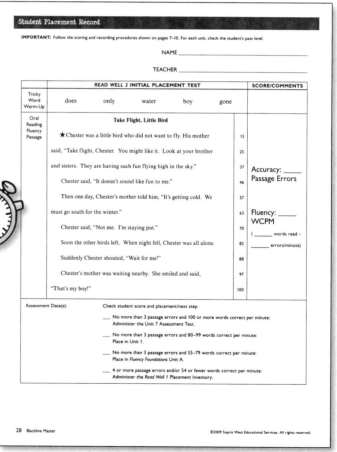

Reproducible Student Placement Record, available on page 28.

Placement System

Administration Guidelines

When administering the Placement Tests:

- assess each child individually, away from others.
- record student responses on the Student Placement Record.
- follow the Administration and Placement Schedule on page 12 or the Summary Flow Charts on pages 13 and 14 to determine placement and/or next steps in the Placement System.

The Placement System tests begin with an unscored and untimed Tricky Word Warm-up, followed by and Oral Reading Fluency Passage scored for accuracy and fluency.

Tricky Word Warm-Up

Have the student point to and read each word. Mark errors on the Student Assessment Record. These errors are not counted against the student.

Oral Reading Fluency Passage

Passing criteria include two measures (accuracy and fluency) for the *same* passage reading.

- **Accuracy:** Number of errors made for the passage

  The accuracy score provides an informal measure of a student's reading level (independent, instructional, frustration).

- **Oral Reading Fluency:** Words correct per minute (WCPM)

  Fluency measures accuracy and speed. WCPM is the number of words read in one minute minus errors for that minute.

Administering the Oral Reading Fluency Test

1. Have the student read the title. The title provides an unscored warm-up.

2. Start timing the passage at the ★. Mark errors using the diagnostic scoring table on page 8. Have the student complete the passage and continue reading for a full 60 seconds.

   - If the student has not completed the passage by the end of 60 seconds, make a single slash (/) after the last word read by the student.

   - If the student finishes the passage before 60 seconds have passed, have the student go back to the ★ and keep reading. Stop the student at 60 seconds and make a double slash (//) after the last word read by the student. On the second pass, mark errors differently (e.g. ✓).

DIAGNOSTIC SCORING FOR ORAL READING FLUENCY ASSESSMENTS

If the student . . .	Then . . .	Record . . .
Needs Assistance	Wait three seconds. Gently tell the student the correct response, draw a line through the item, and write an "A" for "assisted." Score as an incorrect response.	Incorrect We could hear my ki/tten ᴬ cry.
Mispronounces or Substitutes a Word or Sound	Draw a line through the word. Record what the student said. Score as an incorrect response.	Incorrect that Where was t/e kitten?
Omits a Word or Word Part	Circle the omission. Score as an incorrect response.	Incorrect The (sad) kitten was in the tree.
Inserts a Word	Write what the student said, using a caret to show where the student inserted the word. Score as incorrect.	Incorrect up Why was she ‸there?
Self-Corrects	If the student spontaneously self-corrects, write "SC" and score as a correct response. If the student requires more than two attempts, score as an incorrect response.	Correct SC went/met We met at noon. Incorrect went/were/met We m/et at noon.
Repeats a Word	Underline repeated words. Score as a correct response.	<u>What</u> could she do?
Reverses Words	Draw a line around the words as shown. Score as a correct response.	She⌐could rest.

SECOND TIME THROUGH

Any Error	Make a ✓ over each word.	✓ Where was the kitten?

How to Administer Oral Reading Fluency Assessments

The following is a sample script for the initial *Read Well 2* Placement Test.

Tricky Word Warm-Up

Tell the student to point to each item and say the word. If students do not know the word, tell them. Say something like:

> Touch under the first word.
> Read the word.

Oral Reading Fluency

- Tell the student to point to the first word in the title. Say something like:

  > Point to the first word in the title. Read the title of the story.
  > What do you think the story is going to be about?

- Have the student point to the first word in the passage. Start the timer as soon as the student reads the first word of the passage. Have the student read the complete passage and continue reading for 60 seconds. Say something like:

  > Read the story to me. Please track the words with your finger so I can see where you are reading. Put your finger under the first word. Begin whenever you are ready. If you finish the passage before I say stop, go back to the star and read it again.

- If time remains at the end of the passage, have the student go back to the ★ and continue reading until 60 seconds have passed. Say something like:

  > Great job! Go back to the star and keep reading.

As the student reads, code any errors using the general scoring procedures shown on page 8.

Important Note: Because the student is being timed, it is important to pronounce any word not identified within three seconds. Quietly tell the student the word, have the student continue, and score the word as incorrect.

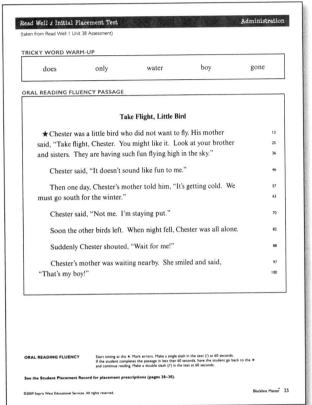

Reproducible *Read Well 2* Placement Test, available on page 25.

Determining Accuracy and Oral Reading Fluency Scores

1. **Accuracy Score:** Count the number of errors made in the whole passage.

   • If the student required more than 60 seconds to read the whole passage, count the errors for the whole passage.

   • If the student read the passage more than once, count the errors only for the first time through.

2. **Oral Reading Fluency Score:** Count the number of words read to the single or double slash. Subtract errors made during the 60-second reading.

Kimora's Example

Kimora's Score

Accuracy

Kimora made 10 errors on the entire passage reading: Chester, flight, such, high, sound, south, Suddenly, shouted, nearby, That's.

Fluency

Kimora read to the word "winter" in one minute (/). During the minute she made six errors: Chester, flight, such, high, sound, south. Kimora read 63 words in one minute minus six errors. Thus, her fluency score is 57 WCPM.

Kimora was assessed for placement in *Read Well 1* as her errors on the whole passage exceeded four.

Student Placement Record

IMPORTANT: Follow the scoring and recording procedures shown on pages 7–10. For each unit, check the student's pass level.

NAME _Kimora_

TEACHER _Ms. Ferris_

	READ WELL 2 INITIAL PLACEMENT TEST		SCORE/COMMENTS
Tricky Word Warm-Up	does only water boy gone		
Oral Reading Fluency Passage	**Take Flight, Little Bird**		
	★ Chester was a little bird who did not want to fly. His mother	13	
	said, "Take flight, Chester. You might like it. Look at your brother	25	
	and sisters. They are having such fun flying high in the sky."	37	Accuracy: _10_
	Chester said, "It doesn't sound like fun to me."	46	Passage Errors
	Then one day, Chester's mother told him, "It's getting cold. We	57	
	away must go south for the winter." /	63	Fluency: _57_ WCPM
	Chester said, "Not me. I'm staying put."	70	(_63_ words read –
	felt/left sc Soon the other birds left. When night fell, Chester was all alone.	82	_6_ errors/minute)
	A said walk/wait sc Suddenly Chester shouted, "Wait for me!"	88	
	Chester's mother was waiting nearby. She smiled and said,	97	
	What's "That's my boy!"	100	

Assessment Date(s): Sept. 12

Check student score and placement/next step

___ No more than 3 passage errors and 100 or more words correct per minute: Administer the Unit 7 Assessment Test.

___ No more than 3 passage errors and 80–99 words correct per minute: Place in Unit 1.

___ No more than 3 passage errors and 55–79 words correct per minute: Place in *Fluency Foundations* Unit A.

✓ 4 or more passage errors and/or 54 or fewer words correct per minute: Administer the *Read Well 1* Placement Inventory.

Reproducible Student Placement Record, available on page 28.

Ralph's Example

Student Placement Record

IMPORTANT: Follow the scoring and recording procedures shown on pages 7–10. For each unit, check the student's pass level.

NAME Ralph

TEACHER Mrs. Ricky

	READ WELL 2 INITIAL PLACEMENT TEST					SCORE/COMMENTS
Tricky Word Warm-Up	does	only	water	boy	gone	
Oral Reading Fluency Passage	**Take Flight, Little Bird**					

Oral Reading Fluency Passage:

Take Flight, Little Bird

that ✓
★ Chester was a little bird who did not want to fly. His mother — 13

said, "Take flight, Chester. You might like it. Look at your brother — 25

and sisters. They are having such//fun flying high in the sky." — 37

Chester said, "It doesn't sound like fun to me." — 46

Then one day, Chester's mother told him, "It's getting cold. We — 57

must go south for the winter." — 63

here
Chester said, "Not me. I'm staying put." — 70

Soon the other birds left. When night fell, Chester was all alone. — 82

Suddenly Chester shouted, "Wait for me!" — 88

His
Chester's mother was waiting nearby. She smiled and said, — 97

"That's my boy!" — 100

Accuracy: 2
Passage Errors

Fluency: 128
WCPM

(131 words read –
3 errors/minute)

Assessment Date(s):
Sept. 12

Check student score and placement/next step

✓ No more than 3 passage errors and 100 or more words correct per minute: Administer the Unit 7 Assessment Test.

___ No more than 3 passage errors and 80–99 words correct per minute: Place in Unit 1.

___ No more than 3 passage errors and 55–79 words correct per minute: Place in *Fluency Foundations* Unit A.

___ 4 or more passage errors and/or 54 or fewer words correct per minute: Administer the *Read Well 1* Placement Inventory.

Ralph's Score

Accuracy
On Ralph's first pass through the passage, he made two errors: put, Chester's. His accuracy score is two passage errors.

Fluency
Ralph read to the word "such" in one minute (//) on his second pass through the passage. During the minute he made three errors: put, Chester's, who. Ralph read 131 words in one minute minus three errors. Thus, his fluency score is 128 WCPM.

Ralph will be assessed on the *Read Well 2* Unit 7 Test for possible placement into Unit 8 or higher.

Reproducible Student Placement Record, available on page 28.

Administration and Placement Schedule

The chart below, the *Read Well* Student Placement Records, and the Flow Charts on pages 13–14 each provide directions for proceeding through the Placement System.

Administer . . .	If the student scores . . .	2nd Grade Then . . .	3rd Grade Then . . .
Read Well 2 Placement Test	54 or fewer WCPM	Administer the *Read Well 1* Placement Inventory.*	Administer the *Read Well 1* Placement Inventory.*
	55–79 WCPM (0–3 errors)	Place in *Fluency Foundations* Unit A.	Place in *Fluency Foundations* Unit A.
	55–79 WCPM (4 or more errors)	Administer the *Read Well 1* Placement Inventory.	Administer the *Read Well 1* Placement Inventory.
	80–99 WCPM (0–3 errors)	Place in *Read Well 2* Unit 1.	Place in *Read Well 1 Plus* or *Read Well 2* Unit 1.**
	80–99 WCPM (4 or more errors)	Place in *Fluency Foundations* Unit A.	Place in *Fluency Foundations* Unit A.
	100 or more WCPM (0–3 errors)	Administer the *Read Well 2* Unit 7 Placement Test.	Administer the *Read Well 2* Unit 7 Placement Test.
	100 or more WCPM (4 or more errors)	Place in *Read Well 2* Unit 1.	Place in *Read Well 1 Plus* or *Read Well 2* Unit 1.**
Read Well 2 Unit 7 Placement Test	99 or fewer WCPM	Place in *Read Well 2* Unit 1.	Place in *Read Well 1 Plus* or *Read Well 2* Unit 1.**
	100–119 (0–3 errors)	Place in *Read Well 2* Unit 8.	Place in *Read Well 2* Unit 8.
	100–119 (4 or more errors)	Place in *Read Well 2* Unit 1.	Place in *Read Well 1 Plus* or *Read Well 2* Unit 1.*
	120 or more WCPM (0–3 errors)	Administer the *Read Well 2* Unit 12 Placement Test.	Administer the *Read Well 2* Unit 12 Placement Test.
	120 or more WCPM (4 or more errors)	Place in *Read Well 2* Unit 8.	Place in *Read Well 2* Unit 8.
Read Well 2 Unit 12 Placement Test	119 or fewer WCPM	Place in *Read Well 2* Unit 8.	Place in *Read Well 2* Unit 8.
	120–140 WCPM (0–3 errors)	Place in *Read Well 2* Unit 13.	Place in *Read Well 2* Unit 13.
	120–140 WCPM (4 or more errors)	Place in *Read Well 2* Unit 8.	Place in *Read Well 2* Unit 8.

* See the *Read Well 1 Assessment Manual.*

** *Read Well 1 Plus* (Units 39–50) and *Read Well 2* Units 1–12 share the same phonics skill sequence. As a core program, *Read Well 2* has a broader range of objectives than *Read Well 1 Plus*. *Read Well 2* includes the introduction of more vocabulary and a wider array of writing activities. The richer units in *Read Well 2* Units 1–12 may require more instructional time than *Read Well 1 Plus* to reach the same level of reading fluency. If *Read Well 1 Plus* is used for third grade intervention, students will be ready for *Read Well 2* Unit 13 upon successful completion.

Flow Chart of Placement Procedures
Grade 2

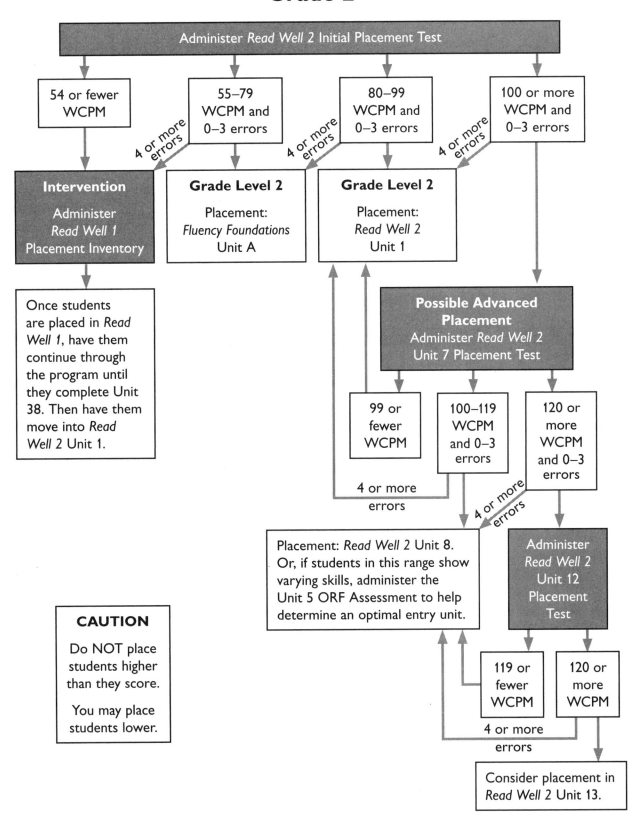

Flow Chart of Placement Procedures
Grade 3 Intervention

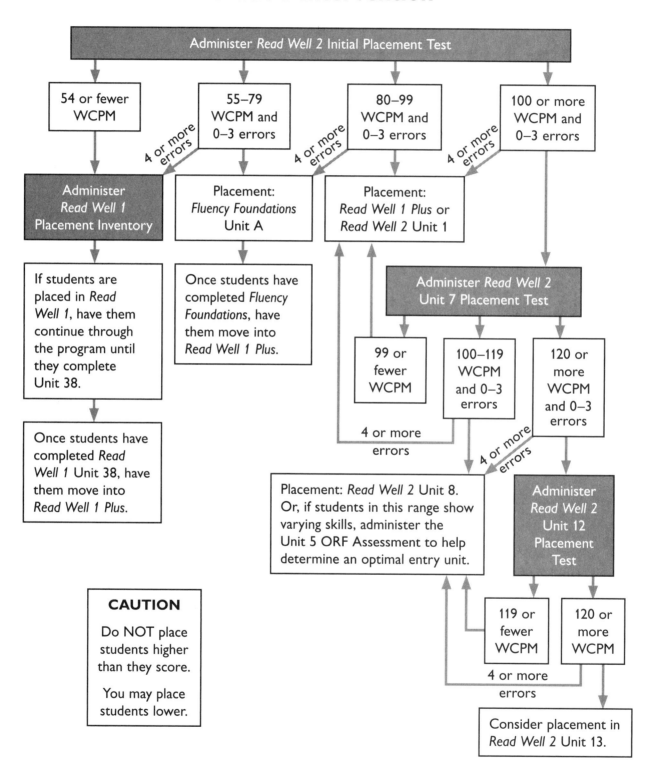

Note: If your school does not have *Read Well 1,* administer the placement test for another focused intervention program. If your school does not have *Read Well 1 Plus,* follow the flow chart on page 13.

Placing Students

Preliminary Decisions

Multiple placement options afford all students individually appropriate instruction and practice *and* sufficient amounts of instructional time. Once all students have been assessed, staff can make preliminary grouping decisions.

Fluency Foundation and *Read Well 2* groups vary in size. Some groups may be as large as 20 students; others may be as small as three. Whether a group is large or small, there will be a range of student skills within each group, but the smaller the range, the better. A group of 15 students with similar skill levels is preferable to a group of three students with divergent skills.

- Determine whether you will group across grade levels or within grade levels. Collaboration is the key to providing every child with developmentally appropriate placement options *and* sufficient amounts of instructional time. Grouping within a classroom is not recommended, because sufficient amounts of instructional time cannot be allocated to each appropriate group.

DEVELOP A COLLABORATIVE READING SCHEDULE

If your school is struggling with how to provide a well-staffed reading block, consider these important options:

a. With administrative leadership, designate uninterrupted reading blocks for each grade level.

b. Collaborate with staff to set up a Walk-to-Read or modified Walk-to-Read schedule.

c. Schedule special education, reading specialist, Title I staff, and other available staff into these blocks of time.

d. Recruit staff members, as needed, to instruct as many groups as possible.

e. Develop procedures for sharing assessment results, regrouping frequently, and sharing instructional strategies. Make a joint commitment to start reading groups as soon as possible and to teach reading every day!

- Determine how many groups your instructional team can teach. *Fluency Foundations* and *Read Well 2* are best taught when each instructional group receives 60 minutes of teacher-directed instruction five days per week. Ideally, low-performing students and students with special needs receive 90 minutes of teacher-directed instruction in two sessions each day. (See *Getting Started: A Guide to Implementation* for information about scheduling and collaboration.)

PLACEMENT GUIDELINES

Place Students Appropriately—Within each group, the smaller the range of student skills, the better.

Teach Collaboratively—Multiple group options allow you to provide individually appropriate instruction and sufficient amounts of instructional time.

Grouping Students

1. Using students' fluency scores (WCPM) from the Initial Placement Test, sort students' Placement Records in descending order, from high to low.

2. Next, sort the students' Placement Records into sets according to where they place (*Read Well 2* Units 13, 8, 5, or 1; *Fluency Foundations*; *Read Well 1* Units 30, 24, 21, 16, 10, 6, or 1).

3. Make a copy of the Group Placement form on page 31. Record student names by WCPM from highest to lowest.

4. Using the ranked scores from the Group Placement form, divide students into groups.

5. Determine where to begin instruction. For each group, start instruction at the lowest-performing students' placement level. For example, if you have a group of six students that includes four students who placed in Unit 8 and two students who placed in Unit 5, begin instruction in Unit 5.

6. Once instruction has begun, adjust groups frequently to meet the needs of individual students.

Roosevelt School Example
See pages 17–23.

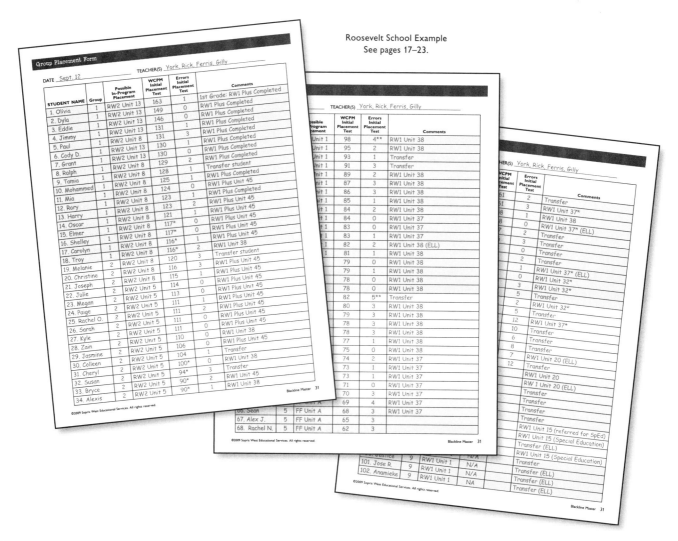

Roosevelt School's Example— Second Grade Collaboration

Roosevelt School is located in a high-risk neighborhood. The staff at Roosevelt has made a strong professional commitment to helping all children read well. Decisions regarding curricula are research based. Decisions about scheduling, staffing, and intervention are based on the knowledge that student success in a high-risk population rests in the hands of a coordinated staff effort. The staff is committed to the following:

- Use of *Read Well K* in kindergarten
- Use of *Read Well 1* and *Read Well 1 Plus* in first grade
- Use of *Read Well 1*, *Read Well 1 Plus*, *Fluency Foundations*, and *Read Well 2* in second grade, as needed
- Use of *Fluency Foundations*, *Read Well 1 Plus*, and *Read Well 2* for remediation in third grade, as needed
- Staff training and coaching in *Read Well*
- Title I and special education staff time scheduled during the reading block
- A 60-minute protected reading block for each grade level
- Options for double dosing in the afternoon

Roosevelt is in its second year of implementing *Read Well*. The staff anticipates seeing stronger readers at each grade level until the first kindergarten cohort reaches third grade. The stable second-grade population at Roosevelt has had *Read Well* in first grade, but not in kindergarten.

Staffing and Scheduling Decisions

The time from 10:00 a.m. to 11:00 a.m. is a scheduled, uninterrupted reading block for the second grade. During this time, the classroom staff, Title I instructors, and special education and ELL teachers provide concentrated small group instruction. The staff implements a walk-to-read model with grouping between classrooms. A Title I paraprofessional, ELL assistant, and special education paraprofessional are available to provide an additional 30 minutes of tutoring or group instruction to second grade students later in the day.

The instructional team meets every other week for the first two months of school and then every third week to discuss assessment results, student progress, and any needed adjustments in student placements.

Administering the Placement Tests

The Title I teacher, special education teacher, paraprofessionals, counselor, and librarian administer the Placement Tests to all second grade students during the first and second weeks of school.

Recording Data

The Roosevelt Assessment Team completes the Placement Tests. Initial Placement Tests are then put in order from highest to lowest and used to make placements. Student names and scores are entered onto the Group Placement Form on page 31 or a computerized data entry form.

Decision Making

By the end of the second week of school, the grade level team and specialists make final grouping decisions. The team weighs and balances the following factors:

- Amount of instructional time per group—Students should receive 60 minutes of teacher-directed instruction five days per week. The minimum time requirement is 45 minutes. Low-performing students should receive a second dose of instruction later in the day.

- Range of skills in a group—Low-performing students should not be placed higher than the placement results indicate.

  If placement options are limited, high-performing second grade students can benefit from *Read Well 2* placements even if the placements are slightly lower than optimum. (Field test results indicated these students were sufficiently challenged, with achievement continuing to accelerate.)

  When compromises are made, students should be monitored carefully. (High-performing students should show continued growth in end-of-unit assessments. Low-performing students should pass end-of-unit assessments.)

- Size of group—the lowest-performing groups are kept the smallest.

- Classroom teachers teach the largest groups.

Resources

Nine instructors are available to teach groups for the reading block. Title I paraprofessionals and the Title I teacher will work as an instructional team, rotating groups.

Teacher	Title
Mrs. Gilly	Second Grade Teacher
Ms. Ferris	Second Grade Teacher
Mrs. Ricky	Second Grade Teacher
Mr. York	Second Grade Teacher
Mrs. Asanti	Title I Teacher, Reading Specialist
Mr. Hamilton	Title I Paraprofessional
Mrs. Hernandez	Title I Paraprofessional
Mrs. Fox	ELL Teacher
Mr. Bennett	Special Education Teacher

Results: the Roosevelt team uses the following placement test results to form initial instructional groups. See page 22 for a summary. The shaded bands show preliminary groups formed by the instructional team.

Group Placement Form

DATE _Sept. 12_   TEACHER(S) _York, Rick, Ferris, Gilly_

STUDENT NAME	Group	Possible In-Program Placement	WCPM Initial Placement Test	Errors Initial Placement Test	Comments
1. Olivia	1	RW2 Unit 13	163	1	1st Grade: RW1 Plus Completed
2. Dyla	1	RW2 Unit 13	149	0	RW1 Plus Completed
3. Eddie	1	RW2 Unit 13	146	0	RW1 Plus Completed
4. Jimmy	1	RW2 Unit 13	131	1	RW1 Plus Completed
5. Paul	1	RW2 Unit 8	131	3	RW1 Plus Completed
6. Cody D.	1	RW2 Unit 13	130	1	RW1 Plus Completed
7. Grant	1	RW2 Unit 13	130	0	RW1 Plus Completed
8. Ralph	1	RW2 Unit 8	129	2	RW1 Plus Completed
9. Tamia	1	RW2 Unit 8	128	1	Transfer student
10. Mohammed	1	RW2 Unit 8	125	1	RW1 Plus Completed
11. Mia	1	RW2 Unit 8	124	0	RW1 Plus Unit 45
12. Rory	1	RW2 Unit 8	123	1	RW1 Plus Completed
13. Harry	1	RW2 Unit 8	123	2	RW1 Plus Unit 45
14. Oscar	1	RW2 Unit 8	121	1	RW1 Plus Unit 45
15. Elmer	1	RW2 Unit 8	117*	0	RW1 Plus Unit 45
16. Shelley	1	RW2 Unit 8	117*	0	RW1 Plus Unit 45
17. Carolyn	1	RW2 Unit 8	116*	1	RW1 Plus Unit 45
18. Troy	1	RW2 Unit 8	116*	2	RW1 Unit 38
19. Melanie	2	RW2 Unit 8	120	3	Transfer student
20. Christine	2	RW2 Unit 8	116	3	RW1 Plus Unit 45
21. Joseph	2	RW2 Unit 8	115	1	RW1 Plus Unit 45
22. Julie	2	RW2 Unit 5	114	0	RW1 Plus Unit 45
23. Megan	2	RW2 Unit 5	113	0	RW1 Plus Unit 45
24. Paige	2	RW2 Unit 5	111	1	RW1 Plus Unit 45
25. Rachel O.	2	RW2 Unit 5	111	2	RW1 Plus Unit 45
26. Sarah	2	RW2 Unit 5	111	0	RW1 Plus Unit 45
27. Kyle	2	RW2 Unit 5	111	0	RW1 Plus Unit 45
28. Zain	2	RW2 Unit 5	110	0	RW1 Unit 38
29. Jasmine	2	RW2 Unit 5	106	0	RW1 Plus Unit 45
30. Colleen	2	RW2 Unit 5	104	1	Transfer
31. Cheryl	2	RW2 Unit 5	100*	0	RW1 Unit 38
32. Susan	2	RW2 Unit 5	94*	3	Transfer
33. Bryce	2	RW2 Unit 5	90*	2	RW1 Unit 45
34. Alexis	2	RW2 Unit 5	90*	1	RW1 Unit 38

GROUPS 1 AND 2

Group 1 will begin at Unit 8. (Six students could begin at Unit 13.)

Group 2 will begin at Unit 5. (Three students could begin at Unit 8.)

If each group were split, teacher-directed time for students would be reduced from 60 minutes to 30 minutes per day—an insufficient amount of time for instruction.

*The lowest students in each group will be given additional fluency practice to even out the range in the group.

Blackline Master 31

Reproducible Group Placement Form available on page 31.

Group Placement Form

DATE _Sept. 12_   TEACHER(S) _York, Rick, Ferris, Gilly_

STUDENT NAME	Group	Possible In-Program Placement	WCPM Initial Placement Test	Errors Initial Placement Test	Comments
35. Michelle	3	RW2 Unit 1	98	4**	RW1 Unit 38
36. Elliot	3	RW2 Unit 1	95	2	RW1 Unit 38
37. Jeremy	3	RW2 Unit 1	93	1	Transfer
38. Jason	3	RW2 Unit 1	91	3	Transfer
39. Leslie	3	RW2 Unit 1	89	2	RW1 Unit 38
40. Destiny	3	RW2 Unit 1	87	3	RW1 Unit 38
41. Alex B.	3	RW2 Unit 1	86	3	RW1 Unit 38
42. Tim	3	RW2 Unit 1	85	1	RW1 Unit 38
43. Sienna	3	RW2 Unit 1	84	2	RW1 Unit 38
44. Zoe	3	RW2 Unit 1	84	0	RW1 Unit 37
45. Anna	3	RW2 Unit 1	83	0	RW1 Unit 37
46. Laila	3	RW2 Unit 1	83	1	RW1 Unit 37
47. Angel	3	RW2 Unit 1	82	2	RW1 Unit 38 (ELL)
48. Brian	3	RW2 Unit 1	81	1	RW1 Unit 38
49. Gary	3	FF Unit A	79	0	RW1 Unit 38
50. Steve	3	FF Unit A	79	1	RW1 Unit 38
51. Rosaria	3	FF Unit A	78	0	RW1 Unit 38
52. Barney	3	FF Unit A	78	0	RW1 Unit 38
53. Charles	4	FF Unit A	82	5**	Transfer
54. Simon	4	FF Unit A	80	3	RW1 Unit 38
55. Aaron	4	FF Unit A	79	3	RW1 Unit 38
56. Richard	4	FF Unit A	78	3	RW1 Unit 38
57. Demetrius	4	FF Unit A	78	3	RW1 Unit 38
58. Calvin	4	FF Unit A	77	1	RW1 Unit 38
59. Tom	4	FF Unit A	75	0	RW1 Unit 38
60. Carol	4	FF Unit A	74	2	RW1 Unit 37
61. Jesus	4	FF Unit A	73	1	RW1 Unit 37
62. David	4	FF Unit A	73	1	RW1 Unit 37
63. Hope	4	FF Unit A	71	0	RW1 Unit 37
64. Mick	4	FF Unit A	70	3	RW1 Unit 37
65. Tony	5	FF Unit A	69	4	RW1 Unit 37
66. Sean	5	FF Unit A	68	3	RW1 Unit 37
67. Alex J.	5	FF Unit A	65	3	
68. Rachel N.	5	FF Unit A	62	3	

GROUPS 3 AND 4

Group 3 will begin in *Read Well 2* Unit 1.

Group 4 will begin in *Fluency Foundations*.

Groups 3 and 4 each include one student who technically places one group lower due to 4 errors. However, each student has a high fluency score. Staff decides the higher placement is warranted. If errors do not drop within the first two weeks of instruction, the students will be moved to a lower group.

The lowest four students in Group 3 are also borderline for placement in Unit 1. Because their errors are low, these four students will be given extra fluency practice and placed in the higher group.

Staff hopes that Group 4 will move rapidly through *Fluency Foundations*.

Blackline Master 31

Reproducible Group Placement Form available on page 31.

Group Placement Form

DATE Sept. 12   TEACHER(S) York, Rick, Ferris, Gilly

STUDENT NAME	Group	Possible In-Program Placement	WCPM Initial Placement Test	Errors Initial Placement Test	Comments
69. Roe	5 (cont)	FF Unit A	61	2	Transfer
70. Brooke	5	FF Unit A	61	3	RW1 Unit 37*
71. Alicia	5	FF Unit A	58	1	RW1 Unit 38
72. Cody R.	5	FF Unit A	58	0	RW1 Unit 37* (ELL)
73. Hugh	5	FF Unit A	57	2	Transfer
74. Nate	5	FF Unit A	56	3	Transfer
75. Maya	5	FF Unit A	58	0	Transfer
76. Angela	5	FF Unit A	57	2	Transfer
77. Jenny	5	FF Unit A	56	1	RW1 Unit 37* (ELL)
78. Ken	5	FF Unit A	55	0	RW1 Unit 32*
79. Elijah	5	RW1 Unit 30	54	3	RW1 Unit 32*
80. Anaya	5	RW1 Unit 30	54	5	Transfer
81. Trinity	6	RW1 Unit 24	52	2	RW1 Unit 32*
82. Charlie	6	RW1 Unit 24	48	5	Transfer
83. Tim	6	RW1 Unit 24	56	12	RW1 Unit 37*
84. Kimora	6	RW1 Unit 21	57	10	Transfer
85. Daniel	6	RW1 Unit 21	48	6	Transfer
86. Jada	6	RW1 Unit 21	40	8	Transfer
87. Jeff	6	RW1 Unit 21	35	7	RW1 Unit 20 (ELL)
88. Jessica W.	6	RW1 Unit 21	33	12	Transfer
89. Matthew	7	RW1 Unit 16	N/A		RW1 Unit 20
90. Michael	7	RW1 Unit 16	N/A		RW 1 Unit 20 (ELL)
91. Jessica S.	7	RW1 Unit 10	N/A		Transfer
92. Travis	7	RW1 Unit 10	N/A		Transfer
93. Chris	7	RW1 Unit 10	N/A		Transfer
94. Angel	7	RW1 Unit 10	N/A		Transfer
95. Jonathan	8	RW1 Unit 10	N/A		RW1 Unit 15 (referred f
96. Ted	8	RW1 Unit 10	N/A		RW1 Unit 15 (Special Ed
97. Raquel	8	RW1 Unit 10	N/A		Transfer (ELL)
98. Jaiden	8	RW1 Unit 10	N/A		RW1 Unit 15 (Special Ed
99. Jose H.	9	RW1 Unit 1	N/A		Transfer
100. Justice	9	RW1 Unit 1	N/A		Transfer (ELL)
101. Jose R.	9	RW1 Unit 1	N/A		Transfer (ELL)
102. Anamieke	9	RW1 Unit 1	NA		Transfer (ELL)

GROUPS 5–9

Group 5 will begin in *Fluency Foundations*. Teachers anticipate a slower pace through *Fluency Foundations* than Group 4 will take.

*Group 5 includes students who did not finish *Read Well 1* in first grade and two students who did not quite meet the criterion for placement. The teacher will carefully monitor the progress of these students and consider switching them back into *Read Well 1* Units 34–38 after finishing *Fluency Foundations* Unit H.

Group 6 will begin in *Read Well 1* Unit 21. Groups 7 and 8 will begin in *Read Well 1* Unit 10. Group 9 will begin in *Read Well 1* Unit 1. Staff will work actively to provide a double dose of instruction for Groups 6–9.

Blackline Master 31

Reproducible Group Placement Form available on page 31.

Summary of Preliminary Placements

The Roosevelt second grade team makes the preliminary placements as follows:

Group	Teacher	Placement
	Mrs. Gilly (2nd Grade Teacher)	
1	18 students	Start at *Read Well 2* Unit 8
	Ms. Ferris (2nd Grade Teacher)	
2	16 students	Start at *Read Well 2* Unit 5
	Mrs. Ricky (2nd Grade Teacher)	
3	18 students	Start at *Read Well 2* Unit 1
	Title I Team (Mrs. Asanti, Mr. Hamilton, Mrs. Hernandez)	
4	12 students	Start at *Fluency Foundations* (accelerated pace)
	Mr. York (2nd Grade Teacher)	
5	16 students	Start at *Fluency Foundations* (slower pace)
	Title I Team (Mrs. Asanti, Mr. Hamilton, Mrs. Hernandez)	
6	8 students	Start at *Read Well 1* Unit 21
	Title I Team (Mrs. Asanti, Mr. Hamilton, Mrs. Hernandez)	
7	6 students	Start at *Read Well 1* Unit 10
	Mr. Bennett (Special Education Teacher)	
8	4 students	Start at *Read Well 1* Unit 10
	Mrs. Fox (ELL Teacher)	
9	4 students	Start at *Read Well 1* Unit 1

Staff anticipates that groups will change, with some students moving up rapidly in response to teacher-directed instruction.

3 Weeks Into Instruction

Group 1: Started at *Read Well 2* Unit 8, 18 Students
Mrs. Gilly's group is beginning Unit 10. She reports that all students are appropriately challenged. Because presentation of work is an issue, Mrs. Gilly is teaching students how to submit neat papers, proof answers, and check their spelling by looking in their books.

Because there was a 50 WCPM spread between her highest- and lowest-performing students, Mrs. Gilly has her three lowest-performing students do ten minutes of Short Passage Practice from the day's story with her. These students have made greater gains in WCPM than the other students in the group.

Group 2: Started at *Read Well 2* Unit 5, 16 Students
Students have successfully completed Unit 6 and are also working on presentation of work, using the same strategies that Group 1 is using. The Exercises and Story Reading seem to be at an appropriate level. Ms. Ferris decides to squeeze in additional Short Passage Practice for two students who seem to have hit a plateau.

Group 3: Started at *Read Well 2* Unit 1, 18 Students
Even though Mrs. Ricky's students are passing their end-of-unit assessments, Mrs. Ricky wants more contact with each student. She decides to have six students reread the story with her every third day. (On their rereading day, Mrs. Ricky reduces written work.) Mrs. Ricky feels like she is getting to know her students' strengths and weaknesses. She decides to meet with each group of six once each week. Elliott is making such rapid gains he is moved to Group 2.

Group 4: Started at *Fluency Foundations* (accelerated), 12 Students
This group is on a 3-day plan and has completed Units A–E. All students except Charles have been able to handle the pace. Mrs. Asanti finds that Charles reads by sight and continues to make many errors. The team decides to move Charles to Group 5 for more practice in each unit.

Group 5: Started at *Fluency Foundations* (slower pace), 16 Students
Mr. York's group has completed Units A–B on 4-day plans and Unit C in five days. Mr. York decides to split his group and conduct two half-hour teacher-directed lessons. When the group finishes *Fluency Foundations*, he will merge the groups back into one group for more teacher-directed time. The team decides to move Sean up to Group 4 because he has made huge gains.

Group 7: Started at *Read Well 1* Unit 10, 6 students
Two students are reviewing units from first grade, and four students are transfer students. Mrs. Asanti finds that students are able to complete units that introduce consonants in two days. The group has completed Units 11–16. Mrs. Asanti is hoping to add a double dose in the afternoon. Her goal is to move these students through *Read Well 1* and directly into *Read Well 2*.

Group 8: Started at *Read Well 1* Unit 10, 4 students
Mr. Bennett's group has many special needs. He is able to complete a review of Units 10, 11, and 12 on 4-day plans. Mr. Bennett decides to have his paraprofessional work with each child individually in the afternoon. His ELL student will work with Group 9 in the afternoon.

Group 9: Started at *Read Well 1* Unit 1, 4 students
Mrs. Fox's group of four ELL students is making good progress. Students have completed Units 1–4 with mastery. In their second dose of *Read Well* instruction, the ELL paraprofessional reviews the day's story and comprehension questions, works on oral language, and guides Comprehension and Skill Work as assigned by the ELL teacher.

SECTION 2

Placement System Forms

This section includes the Placement Tests and record-keeping forms.

Permission to reprint the Placement System forms is provided on the copyright page of this manual.

(taken from the *Read Well 1* Unit 38 Assessment)

TRICKY WORD WARM-UP

| does | only | water | boy | gone |

ORAL READING FLUENCY PASSAGE

Take Flight, Little Bird

★Chester was a little bird who did not want to fly. His mother   13
said, "Take flight, Chester. You might like it. Look at your brother   25
and sisters. They are having such fun flying high in the sky."   37

Chester said, "It doesn't sound like fun to me."   46

Then one day, Chester's mother told him, "It's getting cold. We   57
must go south for the winter."   63

Chester said, "Not me. I'm staying put."   70

Soon the other birds left. When night fell, Chester was all alone.   82

Suddenly Chester shouted, "Wait for me!"   88

Chester's mother was waiting nearby. She smiled and said,   97
"That's my boy!"   100

ORAL READING FLUENCY   Start timing at the ★. Mark errors. Make a single slash in the text (/) at 60 seconds.
If the student completes the passage in less than 60 seconds, have the student go back to the ★
and continue reading. Make a double slash (//) in the text at 60 seconds.

See the Student Placement Record for placement test prescriptions (page 28).

TRICKY WORD AND FOCUS SKILL WARM-UP

Hawaii	pencil	thought	snorkel	squawked	adventure

ORAL READING FLUENCY PASSAGE

To Hawaii and Back Home

★Miss Tam had a great time in Hawaii. She learned to dance   12
and snorkel. She visited a volcano and the rain forest. She went   24
many places and made new friends.   30

Going home was bittersweet. Miss Tam was sad to leave her   41
new friends, but she was happy to be going home.   51

When Miss Tam got home, Minnie Bird squawked, "Hello."   60
Then Old Scraggly Cat jumped into Miss Tam's arms. Miss Tam   71
said, "Oh, how nice to be at home!" She had a big smile on her face.   87

For dinner, Miss Tam had red beans and rice. The next day, she   100
got on the city bus. She went to the library to see her friends. She   115
told them all about Hawaii. They thought the party in the garage was   128
strange. Everyone was excited to hear about Miss Tam's adventure.   138

ORAL READING FLUENCY   Start timing at the ★. Mark errors. Make a single slash in the text (/) at 60 seconds.
If the student completes the passage in less than 60 seconds, have the student go back to the ★
and continue reading. Make a double slash (//) in the text at 60 seconds.

See the Student Placement Record for placement prescriptions (page 29).

TRICKY WORD AND FOCUS SKILL WARM-UP

imagine	heard	straight	toward	reptile	Pteranodon

ORAL READING FLUENCY PASSAGE

Franny and Paul

★What would Pteranodons say if they could talk? Let's imagine.   10

"How are your babies, Franny?" asked Paul. The two reptiles were   21
soaring through the air. They glanced down at the nests in the valley.   34

"My babies are growing. I am bringing them plants to eat," said   46
Franny proudly. Franny shouted to her babies, "I'm coming! Food's on   57
the way!"   59

Franny pointed her head toward the nest. Paul said, "Soon they   70
will be ready to get their own food."   78

Paul spread his giant wings again. He started to fly away when he   91
saw a horrible sight. A stampede! Hundreds of dinosaurs were   101
scrambling through the valley. They were in a panic. Paul heard a loud   114
roar. It was Rex, the meat-eating dinosaur everyone feared.   124

"Hurry home!" said Paul to Franny. "Rex is hunting!" Franny   134
nodded and flew straight down to her nest.   142

ORAL READING FLUENCY   Start timing at the ★. Mark errors. Make a single slash in the text (/) at 60 seconds.
                                If the student completes the passage in less than 60 seconds, have the student go back to the ★
                                and continue reading. Make a double slash in the text (//) in the text at 60 seconds.

See the Student Placement Record for placement prescriptions (page 30).

Blackline Master **27**

IMPORTANT: Follow the scoring and recording procedures shown on pages 7–10. For each unit, check the student's pass level.

NAME _____

TEACHER _____

	READ WELL 2 INITIAL PLACEMENT TEST		SCORE/COMMENTS
Tricky Word Warm-Up	does only water boy gone		
Oral Reading Fluency Passage	**Take Flight, Little Bird** ★Chester was a little bird who did not want to fly. His mother said, "Take flight, Chester. You might like it. Look at your brother and sisters. They are having such fun flying high in the sky." Chester said, "It doesn't sound like fun to me." Then one day, Chester's mother told him, "It's getting cold. We must go south for the winter." Chester said, "Not me. I'm staying put." Soon the other birds left. When night fell, Chester was all alone. Suddenly Chester shouted, "Wait for me!" Chester's mother was waiting nearby. She smiled and said, "That's my boy!"	13 25 37 46 57 63 70 82 88 97 100	Accuracy: _____ Passage Errors Fluency: _____ WCPM (_____ words read – _____ errors/minute)

Assessment Date(s): _____

Check student score and placement/next step

___ No more than 3 passage errors and 100 or more words correct per minute:
Administer the Unit 7 Assessment Test.

___ No more than 3 passage errors and 80–99 words correct per minute:
Place in Unit 1.

___ No more than 3 passage errors and 55–79 words correct per minute:
Place in *Fluency Foundations* Unit A.

___ 4 or more passage errors and/or 54 or fewer words correct per minute:
Administer the *Read Well 1* Placement Inventory.

IMPORTANT: Follow the scoring and recording procedures shown on pages 7–10. For each unit, check the student's pass level.

NAME _____

TEACHER _____

	UNIT 7 PLACEMENT TEST		SCORE/COMMENTS
Tricky Word Warm-Up	Hawaii pencil thought snorkel squawked adventure		
Oral Reading Fluency Passage	**To Hawaii and Back Home**		
	★Miss Tam had a great time in Hawaii. She learned to dance	12	
	and snorkel. She visited a volcano and the rain forest. She went	24	
	many places and made new friends.	30	
	Going home was bittersweet. Miss Tam was sad to leave her	41	**Accuracy:** _____
	new friends, but she was happy to be going home.	51	**Passage Errors**
	When Miss Tam got home, Minnie Bird squawked, "Hello."	60	
	Then Old Scraggly Cat jumped into Miss Tam's arms. Miss Tam	71	**Fluency:** _____
	said, "Oh, how nice to be at home!" She had a big smile on her face.	87	**WCPM**
	For dinner, Miss Tam had red beans and rice. The next day, she	100	(_____ words read –
	got on the city bus. She went to the library to see her friends. She	115	_____ errors/minute)
	told them all about Hawaii. They thought the party in the garage was	128	
	strange. Everyone was excited to hear about Miss Tam's adventure.	138	

Assessment Date(s): _____   Check student score and placement/next step

_____ No more than 3 passage errors and 120 or more words correct per minute:
Administer the Unit 12 Test.

_____ No more than 3 passage errors and 100–119 words correct per minute:
Place in Unit 8, or see the Administration and Placement Schedule and/or the Flow Charts
of Placement Procedures on pages 12–14 for alternative placement suggestions.

_____ 4 or more passage errors and/or 99 or fewer words correct per minute:
Place in Unit 1.

IMPORTANT: Follow the scoring and recording procedures shown on pages 7–10. For each unit, check the student's pass level.

NAME _____

TEACHER _____

	UNIT 12 PLACEMENT TEST		SCORE/COMMENTS
Tricky Word Warm-Up	imagine heard straight toward reptile Pteranodon		
Oral Reading Fluency Passage	Franny and Paul		
	★ What would Pteranodons say if they could talk? Let's imagine.	10	
	"How are your babies, Franny?" asked Paul. The two reptiles were	21	
	soaring through the air. They glanced down at the nests in the valley.	34	
	"My babies are growing. I am bringing them plants to eat," said	46	Accuracy: _____ Passage Errors
	Franny proudly. Franny shouted to her babies, "I'm coming! Food's on	57	
	the way!"	59	
	Franny pointed her head toward the nest. Paul said, "Soon they	70	
	will be ready to get their own food."	78	Fluency: _____ WCPM
	Paul spread his giant wings again. He started to fly away when he	91	(_____ words read –
	saw a horrible sight. A stampede! Hundreds of dinosaurs were	101	_____ errors/minute)
	scrambling through the valley. They were in a panic. Paul heard a loud	114	
	roar. It was Rex, the meat-eating dinosaur everyone feared.	124	
	"Hurry home!" said Paul to Franny. "Rex is hunting!" Franny	134	
	nodded and flew straight down to her nest.	142	

Assessment Date(s):	Check student score and placement/next step
	___ No more than 3 passage errors and 120 or more words correct per minute: Place in Unit 13.
	___ 4 or more passage errors and 119 or fewer words correct per minute: Place in Unit 8.

Group Placement Form

DATE _____   TEACHER(S) _____

STUDENT NAME	Group	Possible In-Program Placement	WCPM Initial Placement Test	Errors Initial Placement Test	Comments

SECTION 3

Ongoing Assessment

This section explains how to use end-of-unit assessments to measure and maximize the progress of each child as he or she moves through the program.

Overview

Frequent assessment is vital to the long-term reading health of each student.

Young students thrive when their lessons are supportive and successful. Because children have a range of background knowledge and respond to instruction differently, it is critical to deliver lessons that are tailored to their needs. At the end of each *Fluency Foundations* and *Read Well 2* unit, you will monitor student progress and adjust instruction, as appropriate.

What Is Assessed

Required Oral Reading Fluency Assessments: At the end of each *Fluency Foundations* and *Read Well 2* unit, students are assessed on an unpracticed Oral Reading Fluency Passage. These assessments provide ongoing progress monitoring.

Results of the Oral Reading Fluency Assessments are essential for diagnosing and determining each student's mastery of newly introduced skills, maintenance of previously learned skills, and fluency on passages that increase in readability from unit to unit.

Optional Written Assessments: At the end of each *Read Well 2* unit (Units 5–24), Written Assessments can also be given. These assessments are group administered and consist of stand-alone passages that progressively increase in readability. The assessment activities mirror the types of activities students complete in their daily Comprehension and Skill Work. The format of the Written Assessments provides informal information about a student's ability to generalize the written comprehension skills and strategies taught in the program.

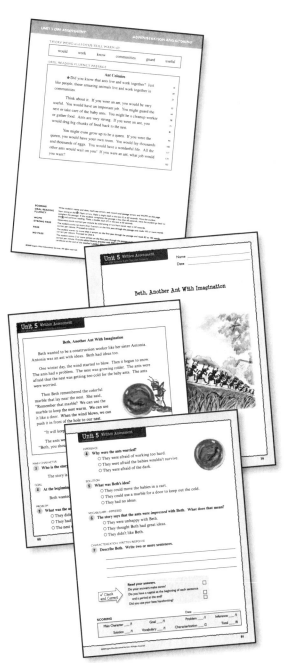

Oral Reading Fluency Assessments

Fluency Foundations and *Read Well 2* Oral Reading Fluency Assessments are designed to monitor progress frequently while protecting instructional time. The Oral Reading Fluency Assessment at the end of each unit takes only a couple of minutes per student and is a quick, reliable form of progress monitoring.

At the end of each unit, you will assess each child individually. The Oral Reading Fluency Assessments will help you determine whether a child:

- is ready for the next unit and the addition of new skills.
- would benefit from Extra Practice lessons.
- needs a quick review to firm up past learning.
- would benefit from a slower pace of instruction.
- needs a faster pace of instruction.
- would benefit from instruction in a different group.

> Be faithful in the administration of the Oral Reading Fluency Assessments. Comprehension is highly correlated with fluency.

UNIT 2 ORAL READING FLUENCY ASSESSMENT   **ADMINISTRATION**
Use after That Kind of Day

TRICKY WORD and FOCUS SKILL WARM-UP

friends	wanted	mother	ordinary	awesome	father

ORAL READING FLUENCY PASSAGE

A Birthday Surprise

★ Today was not an ordinary day for Maya. It was her   11
birthday! Maya's mom said she could play with her best friends   22
all day.   24

Maya looked out at the dark clouds. Rain began to fall.   35
"Oh, no," said Maya. "This is awful!"   42

Maya didn't want it to rain on her birthday. She wanted it   54
to be sunny so she could play with her friends outside.   65

Maya's mother said, "Don't be sad. It will stop raining   75
soon."   76

Maya waited. Her friends came. They had a lot of fun   87
drawing pictures. They played games and they ate birthday cake.   97
The sun came out. Everyone went outside and shouted "Happy   107
birthday. Happy birthday!"   110

Maya smiled. Then she saw her grandfather. "Awesome!   118
You came!" said Maya. "What a perfect birthday." Granddad   127
gave Maya a big hug.   132

ORAL READING FLUENCY	Start timing at the ★. Mark errors. Make a single slash in the text (/) at 60 seconds. Have the student complete the passage. If the student completes the passage in less than 60 seconds, have the student go back to the ★ and continue reading. Make a double slash (//) in the text at 60 seconds.
WCPM	Determine words correct per minute by subtracting errors from words read in 60 seconds.
STRONG PASS	The student scores no more than 2 errors on the first pass through the passage and reads 101 or more words correct per minute. Proceed to Unit 3.
PASS	The student scores no more than 2 errors on the first pass through the passage and reads 80 to 100 words correct per minute. Proceed to Unit 3.
NO PASS	The student scores 3 or more errors on the first pass through the passage and/or reads 79 or fewer words correct per minute. Provide added fluency practice with RW2 Unit 2 Extra Practice. (Lessons follow the certificate at the end of the teacher's guide). After completing the Extra Practice, retest the student.

What Is Assessed
The Oral Reading Fluency Assessments evaluate:

- knowledge of recently introduced regular and Tricky Words.
- oral reading fluency (words correct per minute).

Who Administers
Any trained professional (e.g., teacher, specialist, paraprofessional) can assess students.

When to Administer
Administer the Oral Reading Fluency Assessments at the end of each unit.

The Oral Reading Fluency Assessments can be administered while other students are working on Comprehension and Skill Work or while other students are reading with partners. The following variables can help teachers maintain ongoing assessment:

- Sufficient amounts of instructional time per group

  (See pages 42–45 in *Getting Started* for a description of walk-to-read models.)
- A reading coach or floating paraprofessionals to help assess individuals
- Trained volunteers who can work confidentially to assist

Starting with *Read Well 2* Unit 5, Oral Reading Fluency Assessments can be administered by each group's teacher while other students complete their Written Assessment.

> **INSTRUCTIONAL GUIDELINES**
> One size of reading instruction does not fit all.
>
> Regular progress monitoring is critical to meeting the needs of all children.

Materials Preparation

1. **Student Assessment:** Make one copy per student of the end-of-unit ORF Assessment. You will use these copies to record and score student responses. (You may wish to place your copies in a small group folder or notebook.)

2. **Group Assessment Records:** Make one copy per group of the Group ORF Assessment Record (or set up a similar database).

3. **Individual Assessment Records (optional):** In addition to the Group ORF Assessment Record, you may wish to keep individual student records. If so, make one copy per student of the Individual ORF Assessment Record.

4. **Trained Testers:** Each person who will administer and score assessments must be trained to do so.

5. **Stopwatches:** Obtain stopwatches for each tester. The Oral Reading Fluency Assessments are timed measures.

6. **Clipboards and Pencils:** Place the unit ORF Assessment on clipboards for each person administering the assessment. Have pencils for each test administrator.

7. **Test Administration Area:** Set up a quiet place to administer the Oral Reading Fluency Assessment. Students should be seated at a desk or table.

8. **Assessments for Administration:** Assessments are located in this manual and also at the end of each teacher's guide. The Oral Reading Fluency Assessments are used for both administration and scoring.

   At the beginning of the year, you may wish to assemble a notebook with a copy of each unit assessment for administration. Students can read from the notebook or the unit Teacher's Guide. Make copies to use for scoring each student's oral reading fluency.

The student reads from a copy of the ORF Assessment.

Score on a copy of the ORF Assessment.

Record assessment scores on the Group ORF Assessment Record Form.

Administration Guidelines

- Assess on the last or next-to-last day of instruction in each unit. (See each Teacher's Guide for sample lesson plans.)

- Assess each child individually where others cannot hear.

- Place the assessment (or notebook) on a desk so that the child can easily point to words.

- Position yourself so the student cannot see you score your copy of the assessment.

- Help the child feel comfortable. Most children enjoy one-to-one time with an adult. Say something like:

  I'm glad I get to listen to you read today.

- Throughout the assessment, compliment the student on things he or she can do. Say something like:

  You read with great expression.

  You knew all the words. You read with 100% accuracy.

  I'm very proud of you.

- Score student responses on your copy of the assessment, adhering to the scoring criteria on page 40.

- Record the appropriate score: Strong Pass, Pass, or No Pass.

- Transfer the student's score to the Individual ORF Assessment Record and/or the Group ORF Assessment Record when time allows.

Administration and Scoring

1. As a warm-up, have the student point to and read each Tricky Word. Mark errors but do not include them in the score. Tell the student the word if the student does not know it.

2. Have the student read the title of the passage and predict what the passage will be about.

3. Have the student point to the first word in the passage and track the text while reading the entire passage. Concurrently, time the reading.

   - If the student has not completed the passage by the end of 60 seconds, make a single slash (/) after the last word read by the student. Then have the student complete the passage.

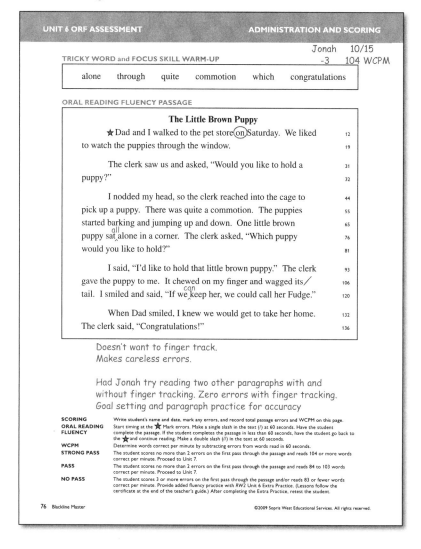

   - If the student finishes the passage before 60 seconds have passed, have the student go back to the ★ and keep reading. Stop the student at 60 seconds and make a double slash (//) after the last word read by the student. On the second pass, mark errors differently (e.g. ✓).

   - As the student reads, code any errors using the scoring procedures below.

4. Record scores. The student's **fluency** score is the number of words read in 60 seconds minus the number of errors made during that minute. The **accuracy** score is the number of errors for the entire passage. If the student completes the passage and begins to read it again, do not count the errors made on the second reading of the passage as part of the accuracy score.

The Oral Reading Fluency Assessments and the Placement Tests are scored using the same procedures. The error criterion for passing an end-of-unit assessment is 0–2 errors—a slightly higher criterion than in Placement Testing (0–3 errors).

DIAGNOSTIC SCORING

If the student . . .	Then . . .	Record . . .
Needs Assistance	Wait three seconds. Gently tell the student the correct response, draw a line through the item, and write an "A" for "assisted." Score as an incorrect response.	Incorrect Alexander said, "I'm a detective." (A written above, line through Alexander)
Mispronounces or Substitutes a Word or Sound	Draw a line through the word. Record what the student said. Score as an incorrect response.	Incorrect Alexander and I went looking for the ring. (were written above "went")
Omits a Word or Word Part	Circle the omission. Score as an incorrect response.	Incorrect My brother Zack came (up) to me.
Inserts a Word	Write what the student said, using a caret to show where the student inserted the word. Score as incorrect.	Incorrect Zack said, "That is ^very funny."
Self-Corrects	If the student spontaneously self-corrects, write "SC" and score as a correct response.	Correct Your ring is in your zipper pocket. (sc / my/your above)
	If the student requires more than two attempts, score as an incorrect response.	Incorrect Your ring is in your zipper pocket. (my/you/your above)
Repeats Words	Underline repeated words. Score as a correct response.	Correct Alexander said, "The case is solved."
Reverses Words	Draw a line around the words as shown. Score as a correct response.	Correct I was happy to have my ring back.

SECOND TIME THROUGH

Any Error	Make a ✓ over each word.	I'm a detective. (✓ over a)

39

ORF Assessment Summary

Readabilities

Fluency Foundations and *Read Well 2* stories were not calibrated for grade level readability, but instead for decodability with the program's letter/sound sequence.

Assessments for *Read Well 2* were calibrated for decodability and readability (Flesch-Kincaid). The assessments gradually increase in readability as shown by the *Read Well 2* Chart on this page. These readabilities do not necessarily reflect a student's grade level reading and may often reflect a low estimate of student abilities. For example, the Oral Reading Fluency Assessment in Unit 13 is 2.7, but the expository selection in this unit has a readability of 4.1.

Fluency Foundations

Unit	No Pass WCPM	Pass WCPM and 0–2 errors	Acceleration WCPM* and 0–2 errors
A	54 or fewer	**55** or more	85
B	59 or fewer	**60** or more	85
C	64 or fewer	**65** or more	90
D	69 or fewer	**70** or more	95
E	74 or fewer	**75** or more	100
F	79 or fewer	**80** or more	105
G	81 or fewer	**82** or more	105
H	84 or fewer	**85** or more	110
I	87 or fewer	**88** or more	110
J	89 or fewer	**90** or more	—

*If the entire group is achieving the Acceleration WCPM, try the 3-Day Plan.

Read Well 2

Unit	Readability (Flesch-Kincaid)	Pass Range WCPM and 0–2 errors	Strong Pass WCPM and 0–2 errors
1	2.0	80–100	101+
2	2.1	80–100	101+
3	2.2	81–101	102+
4		no assessment	
5	2.2	82–102	103+
6	2.3	84–103	104+
7	2.3	85–105	106+
8	2.4	86–106	107+
9	2.4	87–108	109+
10	2.5	88–109	110+
11	2.5	89–110	111+
12	2.6	91–111	112+
13	2.7	93–113	114+
14	2.7	94–114	115+
15	2.8	95–114	116+
16	2.8	97–117	118+
17	2.9	98–118	119+
18	2.9	99–119	120+
19	3.0	101–121	122+
20	3.1	102–122	123+
21	3.2	104–124	125+
22	3.3	106–125	126+
23	3.3	107–127	128+
24	3.4	110–130	131+
25	3.5	112–132	133+

Group Assessment Records

The Group Assessment Records located on pages 97–98 and 100–104 allow you to see the range in your group and prompts appropriate regrouping, acceleration, and/or added practice for some students.

Fluency Foundations Group ORF Assessment Record

INSTRUCTOR: _Mr. York_

Unit		A		B		C		D		E	
Assessment Date		9-15/9-18		9-24/9-25		9-30/10-1		10-6/10-7		10-16/10-17	
Goal Pass		WCPM 55	ERRORS 0–2	WCPM 60	ERRORS 0–2	WCPM 65	ERRORS 0–2	WCPM 70	ERRORS 0–2	WCPM 75	ERRORS 0–2
Acceleration		85		85		90		95		100	
1. Tony	(Placement) (69/4)	69/78	(5)/1	76	2	79	0	88	0	77	0
2. Sean	(68/3)	(54)/74	(5)/3	73	2	85	1	90	2	92	0
3. Alex J.	(65/3)	63/66	(6)/2	83	2	75	0	79	2	83	1
4. Rachel N.	(62/3)	60	1	62	1	Ab		73	1	78	0
5. Roe	(61/2)	63/93	(5)/2	68	2	(64)/75	2/0	78	2	80	2
6. Brooke	(61/3)	(54)/74	(5)/1	73	2	71	2	(57)/69	1/0	76	1
7. Alicia	(58/1)	(53)/67	(3)/1	69	1	(64)/68	1/2	(56)/75	2/0	76	0
8. Cody	(58/0)	55	2	60	0	(64)/66	2/2	(55)/74	0/1	(64)/76	1/0
9. Hugh	(57/2)	58	(3)	63	1	65	0	(58)/70	1/0	(70)/78	2/1
10. Nate	(56/3)	Ab		(58)/65	2/1	66	2	80	0	81	0
11. Maya	(58/0)	71/76	(4)/2	72	0	67	0	72	0	78	0
12. Angela	(57/2)	62	1	65	2	(63)/71	(3)/1	75	1	79	0
13. Jenny	(56/1)	60	2	67	1	74	0	81	1	84	0
14. Ken	(55/0)	55	1	(59)/62	2/1	66	2	73	2	77	2
15. Elijah	(54/3)	59	1	64	1	72	0	74	2	79	1

Comments Unit A · Extra Practice 1, 2, 3 and retest due to errors
Unit B · 4-day unit okay
Unit B · 4-day unit okay
Unit D · Add practice for Brook, Alicia, Cody, Hugh/AmeriCorps volunteer
Unit E · Move Sean to Group 4; reteach group with Extra Practice and retest

Blackline Master 97

Individual ORF Assessment Records

Read Well 2 provides an Individual ORF Assessment Record that allows you to track each student's progress from unit to unit. It documents both accuracy and oral reading fluency scores.

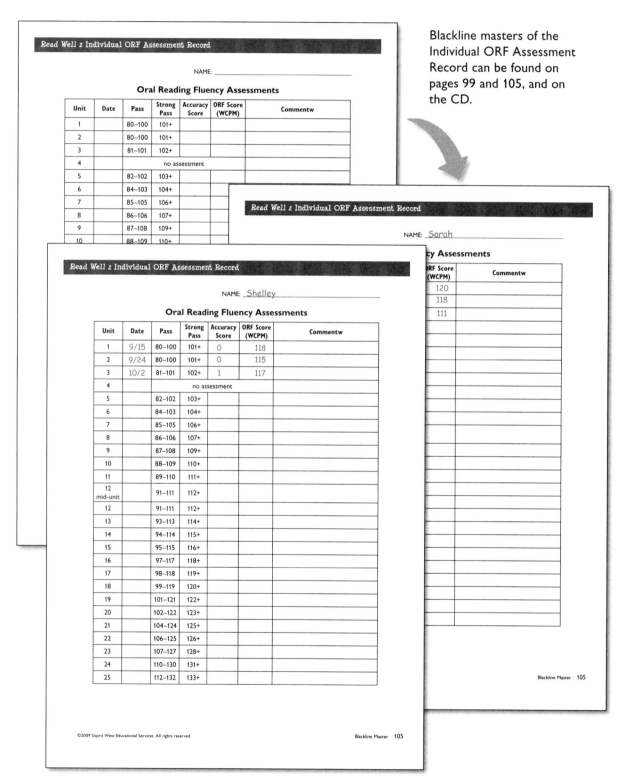

Blackline masters of the Individual ORF Assessment Record can be found on pages 99 and 105, and on the CD.

Read Well 2 Individual ORF Assessment Record

NAME: _____

Oral Reading Fluency Assessments

Unit	Date	Pass	Strong Pass	Accuracy Score	ORF Score (WCPM)	Commentw
1		80–100	101+			
2		80–100	101+			
3		81–101	102+			
4		no assessment				
5		82–102	103+			
6		84–103	104+			
7		85–105	106+			
8		86–106	107+			
9		87–108	109+			
10		88–109	110+			

Read Well 2 Individual ORF Assessment Record

NAME: Sarah

cy Assessments

ORF Score (WCPM)	Commentw
120	
118	
111	

Read Well 2 Individual ORF Assessment Record

NAME: Shelley

Oral Reading Fluency Assessments

Unit	Date	Pass	Strong Pass	Accuracy Score	ORF Score (WCPM)	Commentw
1	9/15	80–100	101+	0	118	
2	9/24	80–100	101+	0	115	
3	10/2	81–101	102+	1	117	
4		no assessment				
5		82–102	103+			
6		84–103	104+			
7		85–105	106+			
8		86–106	107+			
9		87–108	109+			
10		88–109	110+			
11		89–110	111+			
12 mid-unit		91–111	112+			
12		91–111	112+			
13		93–113	114+			
14		94–114	115+			
15		95–115	116+			
16		97–117	118+			
17		98–118	119+			
18		99–119	120+			
19		101–121	122+			
20		102–122	123+			
21		104–124	125+			
22		106–125	126+			
23		107–127	128+			
24		110–130	131+			
25		112–132	133+			

Blackline Master 105

Blackline Master 105

Written Assessments (optional)

Starting with Unit 5, *Read Well 2* includes optional Written Assessments that can provide additional information about a student's progress. These assessments are given at the completion of a unit. Teachers may choose to use these assessments as Comprehension and Skill Activities for the last day of the unit or opt to administer these activities as an informal group assessment.

The written assessments provide information about a student's ability to work independently. They also provide an opportunity for students to frequently practice taking tests.

The results of the Written Assessments should NOT be used to determine whether a student moves to the next unit, but they will show whether a student:

- can comprehend basic story and passage information independently.

- can use new vocabulary.

- can use and generalize comprehension skills and strategies.

- would benefit from more guided practice in their Comprehension and Skill Work.

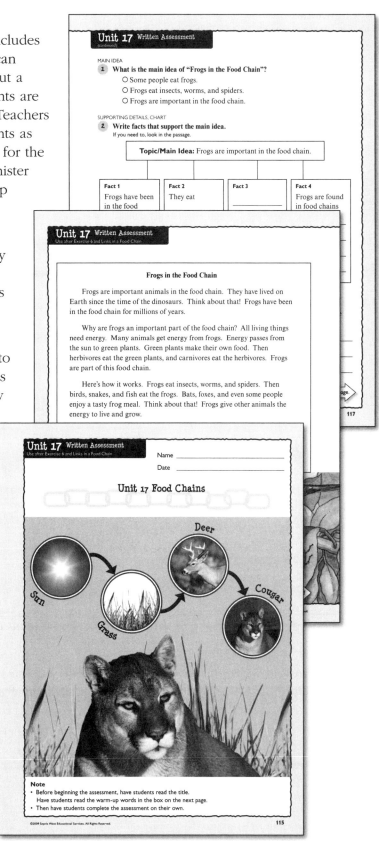

What Is Assessed

The Written Assessments provide information on a student's ability to independently:

- read fiction and nonfiction passages.
- answer literal and inferential questions.
- identify basic story elements: main character, narrator, setting, problem, action, conclusion.
- describe a sequence of events.
- write a retell.
- identify basic expository text elements: topic, main idea, supporting details, and facts.
- write a fact summary.
- use new vocabulary.
- use graphic organizers.
- draw conclusions.
- communicate personal responses.
- identify cause and effect.
- ask questions.

Who Administers

The Written Assessments can be administered to the group by the group's teacher.

When to Administer

The Written Assessments are administered on the last day of each unit in *Read Well 2* Units 5–24. These assessments are given in the place of Comprehension and Skill Work and require about 20 minutes to complete. (No time limit is set.)

Materials Preparation

1. **Student Assessments:** If you are using Activity Books, the Written Assessments are located in the back of each Activity Book. If you are using blackline masters, make one copy per student of the end-of-unit assessment. (You may wish to copy the four pages as 8.5 x 11 inch folders.)

2. **Individual Written Assessment Records (optional):** You may wish to keep individual student records. If so, make one copy per student of the Individual Written Assessment Record.

Scoring

The teacher's guide for each unit includes an answer key. The answer key shows the point value for each item. When responses are open-ended or have multiple responses, the answer key indicates that you should "accept any reasonable response." A scoring summary is provided on the last page of each Written Assessment.

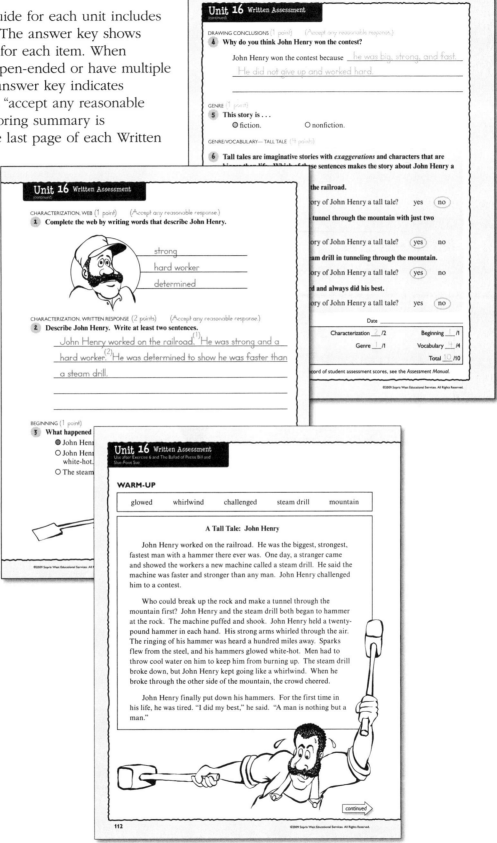

Unit 16 Written Assessment
(continued)

DRAWING CONCLUSIONS (1 point) (Accept any reasonable response.)

4 Why do you think John Henry won the contest?

John Henry won the contest because *he was big, strong, and fast.*
He did not give up and worked hard.

GENRE (1 point)

5 This story is . . .
○ fiction.   ○ nonfiction.

GENRE/VOCABULARY— TALL TALE (4 points)

6 Tall tales are imaginative stories with *exaggerations* and characters that are ~~bigger than life.~~ Which of these sentences makes the story about John Henry a

the railroad.

ory of John Henry a tall tale?   yes   (no)

tunnel through the mountain with just two

ory of John Henry a tall tale?   (yes)   no

am drill in tunneling through the mountain.

ory of John Henry a tall tale?   (yes)   no

d and always did his best.

ory of John Henry a tall tale?   yes   (no)

Date _____

Characterization	2 /2	Beginning	__ /1
Genre	1 /1	Vocabulary	4 /4
		Total	10 /10

cord of student assessment scores, see the *Assessment Manual.*

©2009 Sopris West Educational Services. All Rights Reserved.

Unit 16 Written Assessment
(continued)

CHARACTERIZATION, WEB (1 point)   (Accept any reasonable response.)

1 Complete the web by writing words that describe John Henry.

strong
hard worker
determined

CHARACTERIZATION, WRITTEN RESPONSE (2 points)   (Accept any reasonable response.)

2 Describe John Henry. Write at least two sentences.

John Henry worked on the railroad. (1) *He was strong and a*
hard worker. (2) *He was determined to show he was faster than*
a steam drill.

BEGINNING (1 point)

3 What happened
  ◉ John Henr
  ○ John Henr
     white-hot.
  ○ The stea

©2009 Sopris West Educational Services. All Rights Reserved.

Unit 16 Written Assessment
Use after Exercise 6 and The Ballad of Pecos Bill and
Slue-Foot Sue

WARM-UP

| glowed | whirlwind | challenged | steam drill | mountain |

A Tall Tale: John Henry

John Henry worked on the railroad. He was the biggest, strongest, fastest man with a hammer there ever was. One day, a stranger came and showed the workers a new machine called a steam drill. He said the machine was faster and stronger than any man. John Henry challenged him to a contest.

Who could break up the rock and make a tunnel through the mountain first? John Henry and the steam drill both began to hammer at the rock. The machine puffed and shook. John Henry held a twenty-pound hammer in each hand. His strong arms whirled through the air. The ringing of his hammer was heard a hundred miles away. Sparks flew from the steel, and his hammers glowed white-hot. Men had to throw cool water on him to keep him from burning up. The steam drill broke down, but John Henry kept going like a whirlwind. When he broke through the other side of the mountain, the crowd cheered.

John Henry finally put down his hammers. For the first time in his life, he was tired. "I did my best," he said. "A man is nothing but a man."

continued

112   ©2009 Sopris West Educational Services. All Rights Reserved.

Individual Written Assessment Records

Student's Written Assessments and records may be kept in an assessment folder or portfolio. An optional Individual Written Assessment Record is available for your use on page 106. Gray shaded boxes show inferential questions. White boxes indicate literal questions. Assessments reflect the types of skills and activities that have been practiced in Comprehension and Skill Work.

Unit 9 Written Assessment
(continued)

INFERENCE (1 point)
6 The story doesn't tell you, but the family knew Spot ate the chicken.
   How did the family know?
   O There was a big commotion.
   O Everyone was upset with Spot.
   ● The family saw Spot under the table.

END-CONCLUSION (2 points) (Accept any reasonable response.)
7 **What happened at the end of the story? Write two sentences.**
   Start with *At the end of the story . . .*

   At the end of the story, the family knew that Spot had eaten the food on the table. They laughed about it. They ate leftovers and pie. They had a great time.

Reread your answers.

✓ Check and Correct

SCORING
    Narrator
    Sequence
Teachers: If you wish to keep

66

Individual Written Assessment Record (1 of 2) NAME: Paige

106 Blackline Master

	Date	Genre Readability	Item 1	Item 2	Item 3	Item 4	Item 5	Item 6	Items 7 and 8	Total
Unit 5	9/27	Fiction, Imaginative 2.2	Main Character 1 /1	Goal 1 /1	Problem 1 /1	Inference 1 /1	Solution 1 /1	Vocabulary • impressed 1 /1	Characterization, Written 2 /2	8 /8
Unit 6	10/5	Fiction, Imaginative 2.4	Main Character, Narrator 1 /1	Topic 1 /1	Goal 1 /1	Action 1 /1	Vocabulary • exhausting 1 /1	Drawing Conclusions 1 /1	Characterization, Written 2 /2	8 /8
Unit 7	10/16	Fiction, Imaginative 2.3	Main Character 1 /1	Setting 1 /1	Vocabulary • fascinated 1 /1	Supporting Details 3 /3	Main Idea 1 /1	Main Idea Statement 0 /1		7 /8
Unit 8	10/24	Fiction, Realistic 2.4	Main Character 1 /1	Beginning 1 /1	Middle 1 /1	End 2 /2	Vocabulary • bittersweet 2 /2	Characterization 1 /1		8 /8
Unit 9		Personal Narrative 2.4	Narrator	Main Idea	Vocabulary • tradition	Vocabulary • commotion	Sequence	Inference /1	End, Written /2	/8
Unit 10		Nonfiction 2.5	Topic	Main Idea	Vocabulary • extinct /1	Drawing Conclusions	Facts /2	Personal Response /2		/8
Unit 11		Fiction, Imaginative 2.5	Narrator	Vocabulary • frantic /1	Problem /1	Action /1	Inference /2	Characterization, Written /2		/8
Unit 12		Fiction, Imaginative 2.6	Main Character	Beginning /1	Initiating Event /1	Inference /1	Middle Action /1	End/Drawing Conclusions /1	Inferring/Fact /1 Personal Response /1	/8

Comments: 10/5 Paige continues to display strong written responses. Handwriting is difficult to read. Tends to rush. 10/16 Writing the main idea was hard. Handwriting and presentation skills are improving.

Gray shaded boxes are objectives achieved through inference.

SECTION 4

Making Decisions

This section explains how to adjust instruction to meet the changing needs of your students. Each segment provides information tailored to the developmental progress of students.

Every *Read Well* teacher is a diagnostician.

Adjusting Instruction

Many factors may affect students' progress—absences, attention span, motivation, and so on. Assessment results will help you adjust instruction and practice to meet the changing needs of your groups and of individual students. Meet with your colleagues frequently to adjust groups.

Options for Adjusting Instruction

Fluency Foundations and *Read Well 2* Oral Reading Fluency Assessment results will help you determine when to:

- accelerate groups and/or individuals.
- develop interventions for groups and/or individuals.

Written Assessment results provide additional information about student progress but should *not* be used to determine how rapidly students move through the program. Poor writing skills should not prevent students from attaining grade-level reading abilities.

Analyzing Scores

Use the Group Oral Reading Fluency Assessment Record to:

- analyze the strengths and weaknesses of a group of students.
- compare the progress of individual students within the group.
- quickly share assessment results with colleagues.
- make regrouping decisions.

(Blackline masters of the Group ORF Assessment Records are on pages 97–98 and 100–104 of this manual.)

> **NOTE:**
> Ms. Ferris has marked high scores with an *. No Pass scores are circled.

Read Well 2 Group ORF Assessment Record

INSTRUCTOR: Ms. Ferris

Unit		6		7		8		9		10	
Assessment Date											
Goal Pass		WCPM 84	ERRORS 0-2	WCPM 85	ERRORS 0-2	WCPM 86	ERRORS 0-2	WCPM 87	ERRORS 0-2	WCPM 88	ERRORS 0-2
Strong Pass		104		106		107		109		110	
1. Melanie (Placement) 120/3		125*	0	122*	0	129*	0	Move up with quick tutorial			
2. Christine 116/3		126*	1	115	0	102	0	109	0		
3. Joseph 115/1		115	1	122*	0	125	0	119	0		
4. Julie 114/0		104	0	128*	0	118	1	129*	1		
5. Megan 113/0		78/116	1/0	116	0	121	0	98	0		
6. Paige 111/1		95	0	100	1	102	1	107	0		
7. Rachel O. 111/2		100	0	107	1	110	1	108	0		
8. Sarah 111/0		114	0	119	0	121*	0	115	1		
9. Kyle 111/0		116	1	103	1	118	2	121	1		
10. Zain 110/0		142*	0	131*	0	138*	0	Move up with quick tutorial			
11. Jasmine 106/0		106	0	106	0	95	0	100	1		
12. Colleen 104/1		104	0	128*	0	118	0	125*	1		
13. Cheryl 100/0		88	0	108	0	106	1	110	0		
14. Susan 94/3		100	0	93/90	(4)/0	97	0	106	0		
15. Bryce 90/2		80/117	1/1	102	0	94	2	(82)	1		

Comments: Unit 6: Retest Megan (bad cold on first test); Bryce: slow but accurate—needs to do homework
Unit 7: Retest Susan and watch
Unit 8: Set up extra Partner Reading for Megan and Bryce

Blackline Master 101

At the end of each unit, review your Group ORF Assessment Record. If you are part of a walk-to-read model, meet on a regular basis to share results, problem solve, and regroup as appropriate. When regrouping, watch for trends. Do not rely on a single score.

GENERAL PRESCRIPTIONS		
When . . .	**Score(s) a . . .**	**Then . . .**
An entire small group	Strong Pass	Continue forward. Consider a faster pace of instruction only when an accelerated plan is presented on the Daily Lesson Planner in the unit teacher's guide. For example, the group could move from an 8-day plan to a 6-day plan.
Individuals within a small group		Consider moving those individuals into a higher-level group.
An entire small group	Pass	Continue forward at the same pace of instruction.
Part of a small group		Reteach using Extra Practice.
An entire small group	No Pass	Emphasize instruction and practice on any difficult skills while: • providing Extra Practice lessons for the unit. • reteaching lessons from the unit. • previewing the next unit. • providing a Jell-Well Review of previous units (see page 59).
Individuals within a small group		Provide a second dose of instruction for these students. Consider regrouping.

STRONG PASS/PASS
Most students will receive Passes or Strong Passes when:
• placed appropriately.
• grouped appropriately.
• given sufficient instructional time.
• taught well.

Double Dosing

Read Well's flexible construction makes it possible to help students become independent readers at an optimal rate. Schools often give low-performing students a double dose of *Read Well* instruction to maximize progress.

A double dose of *Read Well* instruction may be provided:

For . . .	By . . .	When . . .	With . . .
• A group • Part of a group • An individual student	• Another teacher (classroom or specialist) • Paraprofessional • Parent volunteer • Older student • Peer	• Before school • After school • During school, outside of the reading block	• Additional *Read Well* lessons within a day • Extra Practice within a unit • Preteaching lessons • Reteaching lessons • Remediation of a skill • Jell-Well Review (cycling back through previously learned lessons)

Note: In some cases, schools intervene aggressively with a triple dose of *Read Well* instruction and practice for the highest-risk students.

Using Oral Reading Fluency Assessment Results

Pass, No Pass

In *Fluency Foundations*, you will find the criteria for a Pass and No Pass at the bottom of each assessment.

PASS	The student scores no more than 2 errors on the first pass through the passage and reads 80 or more words correct per minute. Proceed to Unit G.
NO PASS	The student scores 3 or more errors on the first pass through the passage and/or reads 79 or fewer words correct per minute. Provide targeted practice, use the Unit F Extra Practice lessons, reteach and/or provide a Jell-Well Review. Then retest.

Strong Pass, Pass, No Pass

In *Read Well 2*, you will find the criteria for a Strong Pass, Pass, and No Pass at the bottom of each assessment.

STRONG PASS	The student scores no more than 2 errors on the first pass through the passage and reads 114 or more words correct per minute. Proceed to Unit 14.
PASS	The student scores no more than 2 errors on the first pass through the passage and reads 93 to 113 words correct per minute. Proceed to Unit 14.
NO PASS	The student scores 3 or more errors on the first pass through the passage and/or reads 92 or fewer words correct per minute. Provide added fluency practice with RW2 Unit 13 Extra Practice. (Lessons follow the certificate at the end of the teacher's guide.) After completing the Extra Practice, retest the student.

ORAL READING FLUENCY

Research has shown that oral reading fluency can be a stronger measure of comprehension than traditionally used classroom assessments for reading comprehension. Fuchs, Fuchs, and Maxwell (1988) found a significantly higher correlation between oral reading fluency and the Comprehension Subtest of the Stanford Reading Achievement Test than between fluency and traditional direct measures of comprehension (e.g., question answering, passage recall, and cloze).

Research Snapshot

Oral reading fluency is a powerful measure of students' reading abilities. Prescriptions for placement, pacing, and instruction are provided in each unit's teacher's guide.

Prescriptions

Strong Pass*

If a group is reading with a high degree of fluency, a faster pace of instruction may be warranted.

Have students set goals. (Until students are reading approximately 180 words correct per minute, oral reading fluency can continue to be an instructional goal.)

When an individual student within a group excels, consider moving the student into a higher-performing group.

> **STRONG PASS**
> Consistent Strong Passes signal the possibility of moving faster.
>
> **PASS**
> A Pass signals an appropriate pace of instruction.
>
> **NO PASS**
> A No Pass indicates the need for immediate intervention.

Pass

Continue with the current pace of instruction. Consider increasing fluency practice.

Some students will need more practice than others in their group to build and maintain fluency, even though they may be reading accurately. Prescriptions include short tutorials and/or a second dose of reading.

No Pass

Errors indicate a need to reteach. However, some teacher discretion is required. If errors are the result of a repeated mistake on a single word or skill, it is appropriate to move forward but reteach the word or skill. Some students have a firm understanding of skills but are careless with reading. Sometimes an increased focus on accuracy will suffice.

Consistently low fluency scores indicate that the student needs more practice on previously learned skills. Re-evaluate placement or provide a Jell-Well Review (see page 60). A Jell-Well Review takes students back to an easier level. The goal is to increase depth of knowledge on known skills. Fluency is difficult to achieve on material that requires skills that are not yet firm.

Fluency Foundations does not include a Strong Pass. If students score at or above the acceleration score (see page 40), consider shortening units by following the 3-Day Acceleration Plans found in the teacher's guides.

Intervention Flow Charts

These flow charts demonstrate how to plan instruction based on student performance and extend practice as needed with each unit's Extra Practice lessons.

Fluency Foundations

For students needing intensive intervention, parallel *Read Well 1* lessons also provide an option for additional instruction and practice. Parallel lessons are listed in each *Fluency Foundations* unit on the title page and the Sequence and Sound Pronunciation Guide.

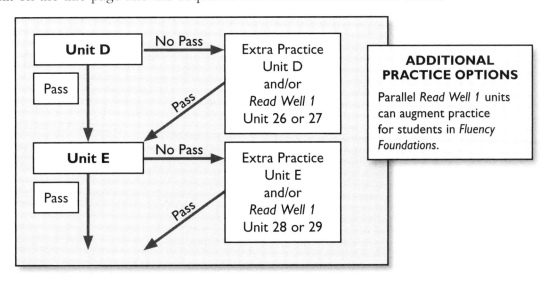

ADDITIONAL PRACTICE OPTIONS

Parallel *Read Well 1* units can augment practice for students in *Fluency Foundations*.

Read Well 2

For students needing intensive intervention in Units 1–12, parallel *Read Well 1 Plus* lessons also provide an option for additional instruction and practice. Parallel units are listed in *Getting Started* on page 31.

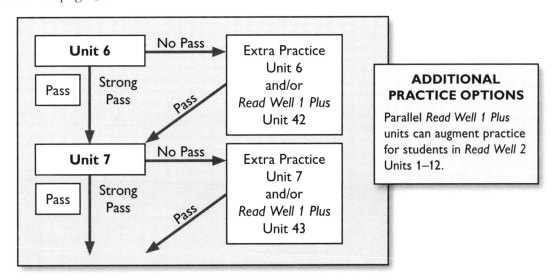

ADDITIONAL PRACTICE OPTIONS

Parallel *Read Well 1 Plus* units can augment practice for students in *Read Well 2* Units 1–12.

Jell-Well Review

If students score a No Pass on two consecutive units, consider a quick review of previous units. See page 60.

Diagnostic–Prescriptive Teaching

	SPECIFIC PRESCRIPTIONS
If students have difficulty with . . .	**Then try these prescriptions . . .**
Reading accurately	Focus on reducing careless errors, repetitions, and self-corrections during oral reading.

Follow these steps:

1. Provide an Extra Practice lesson. (For Units 1–12, *Read Well 1 Plus* units may be used to provide extra practice.)

   a. After students read the passage, have children listen to you read. Tell students that they can raise their hands (or mark their stories with a simple slash) when they hear you make an error. Model each of the following types of errors:
      • Reading a word incorrectly
      • Leaving out a word

      Explain that it is important to read words accurately and only once. Tell students they should also count the following as errors:
      • Making corrections
      • Repeating a word

   b. Read the passage slowly. Make errors and ham it up. The children will love catching your errors.

   c. Have students read the passage with individual turns on sentences. Quietly count errors.

   d. Review the errors without identifying individuals. Have students practice reading the sentences accurately.

   e. Have students reread the passage. The goal is to improve students' accuracy.

   f. Acknowledge accomplishments. Say things like: Wow, you read two paragraphs carefully.

2. Give students individual turns when they finger track. Say things like: [Jack], you get to read the next two sentences. You had your finger on the words, and you are reading each word carefully.

3. Have students set group and individual goals. Say things like: You read page 13 with only two mistakes—"the" instead of "a" and "walk" instead of "walking." Do you think we can read the next page with only one mistake?

SPECIFIC PRESCRIPTIONS

If students have difficulty with . . .	Then try these prescriptions . . .
Tricky Words	1. To correct common errors (e.g., reading "what" for "that," "where" for "there," or "and" for "said"), have the group orally spell the word with letter names. For minimal pairs, such as errors on "where" and "were," emphasize the letter that makes the difference. For example, write "wHere" on the board. Have the group orally spell "where," saying the letter <u>H</u> loudly. Then have students write three questions with "where." Repeat practice each day.

2. For students in *Fluency Foundation*, have students practice reading the Tricky Words on the back of their Homework on a daily basis.

   Do not have *Fluency Foundations* students practice from generic high-frequency word lists. In *Fluency Foundations*, high-frequency words are taught in sequence with the sounds taught. High-frequency words—irregular words—are introduced gradually and within the letter/sound sequence, even though irregular.

3. For students in *Read Well 2*, provide additional daily practice reading the Tricky Words on the Word Fluencies. Word Fluency BLMs are provided on the CD for Units 1–19.

   • To build accuracy, have students read High-Frequency Tricky Words with partners.

   • To build fluency, have students read High-Frequency Tricky Words three times in a row. |
| Fluency | 1. Extend lessons (e.g., if students are working on 6-Day Plans, implement 8-Day Plans). Spend more time on repeated readings of stories.

   • After practicing the story with choral reading and individual turns on sentences, give each student a turn to read a page.

   • Set an accuracy goal of 0–2 errors.

   • To motivate practice, give each student a transparency and a marker. Have students follow along and mark errors as individuals take turns.

   • Have the strongest reader read first. Model giving compliments.

   • Have one or two students give a compliment to each child.

   • Congratulate the child each time his or her fluency improves. |

(continued)

SPECIFIC PRESCRIPTIONS

If students have difficulty with . . .	Then try these prescriptions . . .
Fluency (*cont.*)	2. Set up extra reading sessions with a tutor. • Set an accuracy goal of 0–2 errors. • Have the student read a previously read *Read Well* Homework story for accuracy or have the student read correlated *Read Well 1* or *Read Well 1 Plus* stories. (*Fluency Foundations* and *Read Well 1* correlations are found in the teacher's guides in the Sequence and Sound Pronunciation Guides and also in *Getting Started* on page 88.) *Read Well 2* Units 1–12 and *Read Well 1 Plus* correlations are found in *Getting Started* on page 89. 3. Set up Fluency Booster Notebooks that include previously read Homework stories. Put the stories in three-ring binders. Begin each day's lesson with a three-minute whisper read from the old Homework stories. Have students mark where they are at the end of three minutes. The next day, the goal is to read farther. 4. For *Read Well 2* students, provide additional practice each day with the Word Fluencies (Units 1–3, 5–8, 10–19). The Word Fluencies are included as blackline masters on the CD. 5. Have students read into a tape recorder then listen to their reading, marking errors on a transparency. Have the student reread until satisfied with his or her recording. 6. Provide additional Short Passage Practice with individuals. • Model how to read a paragraph with expression. • Reread the paragraph with the student. • Have the student reread the paragraph.

Appropriate practice makes perfect.

Using Written Assessment Results

If students pass the Oral Reading Fluency Assessment, they should continue forward with the next unit. If any student has difficulty with the Written Assessment, re-administer the assessment orally.

Some students may comprehend well but have difficulty responding in writing.

SPECIFIC PRESCRIPTIONS

Try these prescriptions if the student is not able to answer questions orally . . .

1. Provide explicit instruction for the types of questions missed during reading group, before independent work, in tutorials, and/or in a double dose of reading.

   - Demonstrate (or model) appropriate responses.

   - Guide practice.

   - Provide opportunities for independent practice. Call on the student to ensure participation.

2. For inferential questions, think aloud with students—explain how you arrive at an answer.

3. For literal questions, teach students to reread a passage, locate information, reread the question, and respond.

4. For selected vocabulary words, preteach or review vocabulary words before story reading. Work actively to have the student or students use these words in oral language.

SPECIFIC PRESCRIPTIONS

Then try these prescriptions if the student is able to answer questions orally but has difficulty with the Written Assessment and assignments . . .

Handwriting Fluency	1. If a student or students have difficulty with handwriting (e.g., drawing letters rather than writing letters with automaticity), provide regular, daily handwriting practice. For example, on written retells:

    a. Have students dictate the response. Write answers on an overhead copy or enlarged copy of the retell.

    b. Make copies of the filled-in retell to use for handwriting fluency practice the next day. Have students trace the retell, using fine marker pens for fun.

2. Have the student or students complete Comprehension and Skill Work orally as appropriate, rather than in writing, while building handwriting fluency skills.

- Have students trace or copy the alphabet on a regular basis.

- Have students trace and then copy the same sentence a couple of times.

- Have students keep a "personal best" writing sample in their reading folder. (Put the paper in a plastic cover.)

Syntax	If a student has difficulty composing a correctly stated answer, have the student orally answer the question.

- Rephrase for the student and then have the student repeat the rephrased sentence before writing it.

- Frame responses to support good sentence structure.

Spelling	If the student or students have difficulty composing a correctly stated answer due to spelling:

- teach students to look for the word they need to spell on their assessment or Comprehension and Skill Activity.

- write word banks on the board for students to use when doing their written work.

- teach students explicity with modeling and guided practice how to do best guess spelling. Write each sound you hear. If you aren't sure how to spell a sound, write a dash.

- long range—implement *Read Well Spelling 1* to complement instruction for low-performing students. (This requires a 90-minute reading/ spelling block.)

Extra Practice

Most children can benefit from more practice, but some children *require* extra practice to master new skills with depth and fluency.

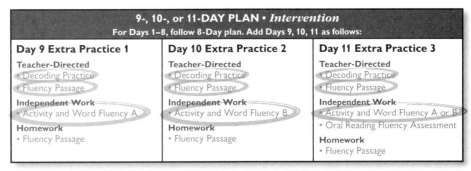

9-, 10-, or 11-DAY PLAN • *Intervention*		
For Days 1–8, follow 8-Day plan. Add Days 9, 10, 11 as follows:		
Day 9 Extra Practice 1	**Day 10 Extra Practice 2**	**Day 11 Extra Practice 3**
Teacher-Directed	**Teacher-Directed**	**Teacher-Directed**
• Decoding Practice	• Decoding Practice	• Decoding Practice
• Fluency Passage	• Fluency Passage	• Fluency Passage
Independent Work	**Independent Work**	**Independent Work**
• Activity and Word Fluency A	• Activity and Word Fluency B	• Activity and Word Fluency A or B
Homework	**Homework**	• Oral Reading Fluency Assessment
• Fluency Passage	• Fluency Passage	**Homework**
		• Fluency Passage

Each *Fluency Foundation* unit includes four Extra Practice lessons. Each *Read Well 2* unit includes three Extra Practice lessons. Each lesson is composed of teacher-directed decoding practice and fluency practice as well as independent work. For ease in planning, Extra Practice lessons are incorporated into the daily lesson plans found in each teacher's guide.

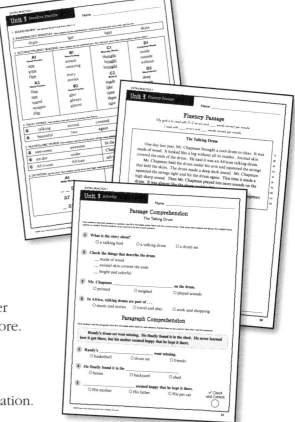

Extra Practice Components

1. Decoding Practice

Sound Review

Review vowels.

Sounding Out Smoothly

Practice skills used for word identification.

Accuracy and Fluency Building

Build automatic recognition of common letter sounds, vowel discrimination, affixes, and more.

Tricky Words

Practice high-frequency irregular words.

Multisyllabic Words

Practice syllable counting and word identification.

Dictation

Practice sounds and onsets and rimes.

2. Fluency Passage

Build accuracy, fluency, and prosody.

3. Activity

Build story comprehension.

4. Word Fluency

Build accuracy and fluency with Rhyming Words, Related Words, and High-Frequency Tricky Words.

AUTOMATICITY

Automaticity is the ability to do something without conscious thought. The goal of the Extra Practice lessons is to help students build automaticity in decoding so that their mental energy is free for comprehension.

Jell-Well Review

Students may periodically need a review of earlier units before they can successfully move forward. A Jell-Well Review helps these students strengthen their foundation, avoid overload, and build confidence. For example, if students do well in Units A–C but require more days to master D, E, and F, you may wish to do a quick recycle through Units C–F to firm up skills before moving to G. Similarly, if students require reteaching and retesting in *Read Well 2*, recycle students through earlier units. For example, if students do well in Units 1–5 but have difficulty passing Units 6 and 7, do a review of Units 5–7 before moving to Unit 8.

How to Provide a Jell-Well Review

To conduct the review, go back to the last unit in which the students received a Strong Pass and review any difficult units. Each day, have students practice:

- sounds learned to date to maintain skills and build fluency.

- decoding words from the review unit to build accuracy and fluency.

- passage reading from the review unit to build fluency.

Option 1:

Use one of the following:

- Extra Practice lessons from the review units

- Decoding Practice and Homework stories from the review units

- Decoding Practice and Homework stories from the *Read Well Plus* units that parallel the review units

Option 2:

Use the Jell-Well Planner found on page 108 to design your own Jell-Well lessons.

Motivation

Young children love routines, but they can also get mired in uninspired practice. Add a few creative twists to maintain motivation. A stopwatch can be used to turn practice into a game. Games can be used if structured for high response rates. Goal setting can be used to motivate them to move quickly through the review.

SECTION 5

Assessments and Forms

This section includes the end-of-unit administration and record-keeping forms.

Permission to reprint the Placement
System forms is provided on the
copyright page of this manual.

ORAL READING FLUENCY PASSAGE

A Sweet Dream

★ Mark had a sweet dream. In the dream, he 9
had a neat cat. 13

Mark and the cat sat near the creek at noon. 23
Mark swam in the stream. The cat swam too. Mark 33
said, "I didn't think that cats could swim! I think this is a 46
smart cat. I want to see what it can do." 56

Soon Mark said, "This cat can do tricks. That cat 66
swam with a swish and a swoosh. I said, 'Start,' and it 78
ran. I could see it dart and dash. That cat can stand. It 91
can wink too. What a smart cat!" 98

SCORING	Write student's name and date, mark any errors, and record total passage errors and WCPM on this page.
ORAL READING FLUENCY	Start timing at the ★. Mark errors. Make a single slash in the text (/) at 60 seconds. Have the student complete the passage. If the student completes the passage in less than 60 seconds, have the student go back to the ★ and continue reading. Make a double slash (//) in the text at 60 seconds.
WCPM	Determine words correct per minute by subtracting errors from words read in 60 seconds.
PASS	The student scores no more than 2 errors on the first pass through the passage and reads 55 or more words correct per minute. Proceed to Unit B.
NO PASS	The student scores 3 or more errors on the first pass through the passage and/or reads 54 or fewer words correct per minute. Provide targeted practice, use the Unit A Extra Practice lessons, and/or reteach. Then retest.

ORAL READING FLUENCY PASSAGE

Shy Rick

★Rick was a shy little raccoon. When Rick was	9
one, he met Kim. Kim was a raccoon too. She was	20
three. Kim said, "Who is this raccoon?"	27
"I am Rick," said the shy raccoon.	34
Then Kim said, "I want to eat."	41
Rick said, "Me too. When can we eat? What can	51
we eat?"	53
Kim and Rick could smell a ham. It was in the	64
trash. Kim said, "Let's eat that ham."	71
A man was near. He said, "Who is there? Who	81
is in the trash?" Then he said, "Scat!"	89
Kim and Rick ran with the ham. "Tee hee," said	99
Rick and Kim.	102

SCORING	Write student's name and date, mark any errors, and record total passage errors and WCPM on this page.
ORAL READING FLUENCY	Start timing at the ★. Mark errors. Make a single slash in the text (/) at 60 seconds. Have the student complete the passage. If the student completes the passage in less than 60 seconds, have the student go back to the ★ and continue reading. Make a double slash (//) in the text at 60 seconds.
WCPM	Determine words correct per minute by subtracting errors from words read in 60 seconds.
PASS	The student scores no more than 2 errors on the first pass through the passage and reads 60 or more words correct per minute. Proceed to Unit C.
NO PASS	The student scores 3 or more errors on the first pass through the passage and/or reads 59 or fewer words correct per minute. Provide targeted practice, use the Unit B Extra Practice lessons, and/or reteach.

ORAL READING FLUENCY PASSAGE

A Grand Team

★It was hard work to be on the team with the   11

Tenth Street Bobcats. The Bobcats ran and ran. The   20

team hit and hit. The Bobcats worked and worked.   29

Beth said, "We should try and be the best team   39

we can be."   42

Matt said, "We need to be strong. Then we can   52

whack and blast that ball."   57

Rod said, "The Tenth Street Bobcats can swing   65

the bat, smack the ball, and win, win, win!"   74

Ann nodded and began to grin. Then she said,   83

"Isn't this a fantastic team?"   88

The team all said, "Go Bobcats! Let's blast that   97

ball!" What a grand team.   102

SCORING	Write student's name and date, mark any errors, and record total passage errors and WCPM on this page.
ORAL READING FLUENCY	Start timing at the ★. Mark errors. Make a single slash in the text (/) at 60 seconds. Have the student complete the passage. If the student completes the passage in less than 60 seconds, have the student go back to the ★ and continue reading. Make a double slash in the text (//) at 60 seconds.
WCPM	Determine words correct per minute by subtracting errors from words read in 60 seconds.
PASS	The student scores no more than 2 errors on the first pass through the passage and reads 65 or more words correct per minute. Proceed to Unit D.
NO PASS	The student scores 3 or more errors on the first pass through the passage and/or reads 64 or fewer words correct per minute. Provide targeted practice, use the Unit C Extra Practice lessons, reteach, and/or provide a Jell-Well Review. Then retest.

ORAL READING FLUENCY PASSAGE

Brothers

★Martin and Bob are brothers. Martin and Bob	8
do different things together.	12
Bob is too little to read, but his big brother reads	23
to him. Bob asks his big brother Martin, "What's this?	33
What's that? When? Where? Why?"	38
At noon, Bob and Martin went fishing. When	46
Bob and Martin were near the stream, Bob asked,	55
"Where's the fish? Look, is that a fish?"	63
Martin said, "That isn't a fish. That's a big black fly."	74
Then Bob asked, "Look, what's that?"	80
He said, "That's a frog on a log."	88
Then Bob asked, "Look, what's that?"	94
At last Martin said, "Bob, that's a fish in the	104
stream."	105

SCORING	Write student's name and date, mark any errors, and record total passage errors and WCPM on this page.
ORAL READING FLUENCY	Start timing at the ★. Mark errors. Make a single slash in the text (/) at 60 seconds. Have the student complete the passage. If the student completes the passage in less than 60 seconds, have the student go back to the ★ and continue reading. Make a double slash (//) in the text at 60 seconds.
WCPM	Determine words correct per minute by subtracting errors from words read in 60 seconds.
PASS	The student scores no more than 2 errors on the first pass through the passage and reads 70 or more words correct per minute. Proceed to Unit E.
NO PASS	The student scores 3 or more errors on the first pass through the passage and/or reads 69 or fewer words correct per minute. Provide targeted practice, use the Unit D Extra Practice lessons, reteach, and/or provide a Jell-Well Review. Then retest.

ORAL READING FLUENCY PASSAGE

Tucker and Pip

★Tuck has fun in his yard. Tuck's sister, Pip, has   10

fun too. Tuck and Pip play in the sand. Grandfather got   21

the sand for Tuck when Mom and Dad adopted him. It was   33

a birthday gift one year ago.   39

When Tuck and Pip play in the yard, Mom works in   50

the garden. There are little trees and plants all across the   61

yard. Mom picks weeds all day. She gets in the muck and   73

mud. Yuck!   75

Today, Pip's dog dashes across the backyard. King   83

is the best dog. He is big and black. He plays in the yard   97

with Tuck, and Tuck hoots and grins. It is a fun day in the   111

backyard.   112

SCORING	Write student's name and date, mark any errors, and record total passage errors and WCPM on this page.
ORAL READING FLUENCY	Start timing at the ★. Mark errors. Make a single slash in the text (/) at 60 seconds. Have the student complete the passage. If the student completes the passage in less than 60 seconds, have the student go back to the ★ and continue reading. Make a double slash (//) in the text at 60 seconds.
WCPM	Determine words correct per minute by subtracting errors from words read in 60 seconds.
PASS	The student scores no more than 2 errors on the first pass through the passage and reads 75 or more words correct per minute. Proceed to Unit F.
NO PASS	The student scores 3 or more errors on the first pass through the passage and/or reads 74 or fewer words correct per minute. Provide targeted practice, use the Unit E Extra Practice lessons, reteach and/or provide a Jell-Well Review. Then retest.

ORAL READING FLUENCY PASSAGE

Camping in the Park

★ My friends, my mother, and I went camping in the   10

park. The park was a mix of green plants and forest. We   22

visited the park in the spring.   28

Mother had filled a box with food. We had lots and   39

lots to eat. Then we ran and jumped on the great big hill.   52

Matt said, "What if this hill was a volcano?" It was just a   65

hill, but it was fun to play.   72

Bill said, "Can you feel the Earth quiver and jiggle?   82

Quick! Run!" We ran about until it was dark.   91

Mother got a big quilt from the car, and we   101

looked at the stars. What fun! I will remember this   111

fantastic trip forever.   114

SCORING	Write student's name and date, mark any errors, and record total passage errors and WCPM on this page.
ORAL READING FLUENCY	Start timing at the ★. Mark errors. Make a single slash in the text (/) at 60 seconds. Have the student complete the passage. If the student completes the passage in less than 60 seconds, have the student go back to the ★ and continue reading. Make a double slash (//) in the text at 60 seconds.
WCPM	Determine words correct per minute by subtracting errors from words read in 60 seconds.
PASS	The student scores no more than 2 errors on the first pass through the passage and reads 80 or more words correct per minute. Proceed to Unit G.
NO PASS	The student scores 3 or more errors on the first pass through the passage and/or reads 79 or fewer words correct per minute. Provide targeted practice, use the Unit F Extra Practice lessons, reteach and/or provide a Jell-Well Review. Then retest.

ORAL READING FLUENCY PASSAGE

The Lost Ring

★I had a ring. I lost it at the zoo. I asked   12

people, "Have you seen my ring?"   18

    Alexander said, "I'm a detective! I will solve the   27

Case of the Missing Ring!"   32

    Alexander and I went looking for my ring. We   41

made a list of where I had been. We looked near the   53

plants. We looked in the weeds. My brother Zack   62

came up to me. He asked, "What are you doing?"   72

    I said, "Alexander is helping me look for my ring.   82

He is a great detective."   87

    Zack said, "That is funny. Did you forget? Your   96

ring is in your zipper pocket!"   102

    Alexander said, "The case is solved!"   108

    I was happy to have my ring back.   116

SCORING	Write student's name and date, mark any errors, and record total passage errors and WCPM on this page.
ORAL READING FLUENCY	Start timing at the ★. Mark errors. Make a single slash in the text (/) at 60 seconds. Have the student complete the passage. If the student completes the passage in less than 60 seconds, have the student go back to the ★ and continue reading. Make a double slash in the text (//) at 60 seconds.
WCPM	Determine words correct per minute by subtracting errors from words read in 60 seconds.
PASS	The student scores no more than 2 errors on the first pass through the passage and reads 82 or more words correct per minute. Proceed to Unit H.
NO PASS	The student scores 3 or more errors on the first pass through the passage and/or reads 81 or fewer words correct per minute. Provide targeted practice, use the Unit G Extra Practice lessons, reteach, and/or provide a Jell-Well Review. Then retest.

ORAL READING FLUENCY PASSAGE

Wiggy Weasel Plays Ball

★My name is Wiggy Weasel. I am a reporter.   9

When I'm not working, I like to play ball. I think   20

my team is the best one in town.   28

My team works hard. We play on sunny days   37

and on cloudy days. We laugh and have a fantastic   47

time. Sometimes it rains, but we play even if the   57

ground is wet. If there is a hailstorm or a strong wind,   69

then we quit.   72

What do I like about baseball? I like playing with   82

my friends. I like the sound of the bat hitting the ball.   94

Whack! Crack! I like running the bases too.   102

Sometimes we travel to a nearby town to play.   111

We don't win every time, but we have lots of fun.   122

SCORING	Write student's name and date, mark any errors, and record total passage errors and WCPM on this page.
ORAL READING FLUENCY	Start timing at the ★. Mark errors. Make a single slash in the text (/) at 60 seconds. Have the student complete the passage. If the student completes the passage in less than 60 seconds, have the student go back to the ★ and continue reading. Make a double slash (//) in the text at 60 seconds.
WCPM	Determine words correct per minute by subtracting errors from words read in 60 seconds.
PASS	The student scores no more than 2 errors on the first pass through the passage and reads 85 or more words correct per minute. Proceed to Unit I.
NO PASS	The student scores 3 or more errors on the first pass through the passage and/or reads 84 or fewer words correct per minute. Provide targeted practice, use the Unit H Extra Practice lessons, reteach and/or provide a Jell-Well Review. Then retest.

ORAL READING FLUENCY PASSAGE

The Best Gardeners

★Chaz is a fantastic gardener. He helps other   8
people with their plants.   12

One day, I wished for a lot of beans to munch.   23
Chaz helped me plant some seeds in a pail. When it   34
didn't rain, I watered the seeds. When the seeds didn't   44
grow, Chaz gave the seeds notes. The notes said,   53
"Little seeds, you must get bigger."   59

I said, "Chaz, that is foolish. Seeds cannot read."   68

Then one sunny day, the seeds began to sprout.   77
I gave them more water, and then I weeded the ground   88
nearby. Chaz sent the little seedlings even more   96
notes.   97

In the spring, there were small beans on the   106
plants. Soon the beans were as tall as Chaz. We   116
were all speechless. Everyone said, "You and Chaz   124
are outstanding gardeners!"   127

SCORING	Write student's name and date, mark any errors, and record total passage errors and WCPM on this page.
ORAL READING FLUENCY	Start timing at the ★. Mark errors. Make a single slash in the text (/) at 60 seconds. Have the student complete the passage. If the student completes the passage in less than 60 seconds, have the student go back to the ★ and continue reading. Make a double slash (//) in the text at 60 seconds.
WCPM	Determine words correct per minute by subtracting errors from words read in 60 seconds.
PASS	The student scores no more than 2 errors on the first pass through the passage and reads 88 or more words correct per minute. Proceed to Unit J.
NO PASS	The student scores 3 or more errors on the first pass through the passage and/or reads 87 or fewer words correct per minute. Provide targeted practice, use the Unit I Extra Practice lessons, reteach, and/or provide a Jell-Well Review. Then retest.

ORAL READING FLUENCY PASSAGE

Chester Likes to Fly

★Chester is a little bird. When Chester was first	9
born, he did not want to fly. Now Chester likes to fly high	22
in the sky. He likes to fly with his brothers and sisters.	34
Chester took a flight over the sea. He could see	44
sand sharks and bright red fish.	50
Chester took a flight over a farm. He could see	60
chickens, cows, and sheep.	64
Chester said, "Now I understand why mother	71
wanted me to fly."	75
Chester said to his brothers and sisters, "Let's fly	84
over the park." Chester liked to see the kids play	94
baseball. "Wow, look at that girl bat the ball," said	104
Chester. "She seems very happy."	109
Chester said, "I like being a bird. I like to fly over	121
the land and the sea. I am happy too."	130

SCORING	Write student's name and date, mark any errors, and record total passage errors and WCPM on this page.
ORAL READING FLUENCY	Start timing at the ★. Mark errors. Make a single slash in the text (/) at 60 seconds. Have the student complete the passage. If the student completes the passage in less than 60 seconds, have the student go back to the ★ and continue reading. Make a double slash in the text (//) at 60 seconds.
WCPM	Determine words correct per minute by subtracting errors from words read in 60 seconds.
PASS	The student scores no more than 2 errors on the first pass through the passage and reads 90 or more words correct per minute. Second grade students: Proceed to *Read Well 2*, Unit 1. Third and fourth grade students: Proceed to *Read Well 1 Plus*.
NO PASS	The student scores 3 or more errors on the first pass through the passage and/or reads 89 or fewer words correct per minute. Provide targeted practice, use the Unit J Extra Practice lessons, reteach and/or provide a Jell-Well Review. Then retest.

TRICKY WORD and FOCUS SKILL WARM-UP

| again | world | because | wouldn't | thought | yours |

ORAL READING FLUENCY PASSAGE

Maya and Ben

★Hi! My name is Maya. I am in second grade, and this	12
year is great. I live in a cool building, and I have two best friends.	27
My mother, my brother, and I live in the perfect apartment.	38
Today, we are going to braid my hair. Life is good.	49
Hi! My name is Ben. When I first started school here, I	61
thought I might not like it. It seemed like everyone was scowling	73
at me. Now I have a lot of friends. We hang out together.	86
Today, Mr. Chapman said that he would begin teaching us about	97
inventors. I'm named after three important inventors, so that	106
should be fun.	109
We think second grade is going to be perfect. We'll play	120
soccer, work on computers, and have a lot of fun.	130

SCORING	Write student's name and date, mark any errors, and record total passage errors and WCPM on this page.
ORAL READING FLUENCY	Start timing at the ★. Mark errors. Make a single slash in the text (/) at 60 seconds. If the student completes the passage in less than 60 seconds, have the student go back to the ★ and continue reading. Make a double slash (//) in the text at 60 seconds.
WCPM	Determine words correct per minute by subtracting errors from words read in 60 seconds.
STRONG PASS	The student scores no more than 2 errors on the first pass through the passage and reads a minimum of 101 or more words correct per minute. Proceed to Unit 2.
PASS	The student scores no more than 2 errors on the first pass through the passage and reads 80 to 100 words correct per minute. Proceed to Unit 2.
NO PASS	The student scores 3 or more errors on the first pass through the passage and/or reads 79 or fewer words correct per minute. Provide added fluency practice with *RW2* Unit 1 Extra Practice. (Lessons follow the certificate at the end of the teacher's guide.) After completing the Extra Practice, retest the student.

TRICKY WORD and FOCUS SKILL WARM-UP

friends	wanted	mother	ordinary	awesome	father

ORAL READING FLUENCY PASSAGE

A Birthday Surprise

⭐Today was not an ordinary day for Maya. It was her   11
birthday! Maya's mom said she could play with her best friends   22
all day.   24

Maya looked out at the dark clouds. Rain began to fall.   35
"Oh, no," said Maya. "This is awful!"   42

Maya didn't want it to rain on her birthday. She wanted it   54
to be sunny so she could play with her friends outside.   65

Maya's mother said, "Don't be sad. It will stop raining   75
soon."   76

Maya waited. Her friends came. They had a lot of fun   87
drawing pictures. They played games and they ate birthday cake.   97
The sun came out. Everyone went outside and shouted "Happy   107
birthday. Happy birthday!"   110

Maya smiled. Then she saw her grandfather. "Awesome!   118
You came!" said Maya. "What a perfect birthday." Granddad   127
gave Maya a big hug.   132

SCORING	Write student's name and date, mark any errors, and record total passage errors and WCPM on this page.
ORAL READING FLUENCY	Start timing at the ⭐. Mark errors. Make a single slash in the text (/) at 60 seconds. Have the student complete the passage. If the student completes the passage in less than 60 seconds, have the student go back to the ⭐ and continue reading. Make a double slash (//) in the text at 60 seconds.
WCPM	Determine words correct per minute by subtracting errors from words read in 60 seconds.
STRONG PASS	The student scores no more than 2 errors on the first pass through the passage and reads 101 or more words correct per minute. Proceed to Unit 3.
PASS	The student scores no more than 2 errors on the first pass through the passage and reads 80 to 100 words correct per minute. Proceed to Unit 3.
NO PASS	The student scores 3 or more errors on the first pass through the passage and/or reads 79 or fewer words correct per minute. Provide added fluency practice with *RW2 Unit 2 Extra Practice*. (Lessons follow the certificate at the end of the teacher's guide). After completing the Extra Practice, retest the student.

TRICKY WORD and FOCUS SKILL WARM-UP

| through | learned | adventure | cute | wade | beautiful |

ORAL READING FLUENCY PASSAGE

Miss Tam's African Adventure

⭐Miss Tam went on a great trip to Africa. It was an 12
amazing adventure. In Africa, Miss Tam learned many new 21
customs. 22

Miss Tam went on a river trip. She saw monkeys, hippos, 33
and beautiful birds. 36

The monkeys were a lot of fun. Miss Tam saw cute little 48
monkeys eating leaves in the trees. 54

The hippos were awesome. Miss Tam saw the hippos 63
near the river. She saw them wade through the mud and then eat 76
the green grass. 79

The birds were colorful. They were red, blue, green, and 89
black. A small bird flew by, but then it landed near Miss Tam. 102
The bird made Miss Tam think about Minnie Bird. 111

Miss Tam would be happy to go back home. She missed 122
her pets, but she had a grand time in Africa. 132

SCORING	Write student's name and date, mark any errors, and record total passage errors and WCPM on this page.
ORAL READING FLUENCY	Start timing at the ⭐. Mark errors. Make a single slash in the text (/) at 60 seconds. Have the student complete the passage. If the student completes the passage in less than 60 seconds, have the student go back to the ⭐ and continue reading. Make a double slash (//) in the text at 60 seconds.
WCPM	Determine words correct per minute by subtracting errors from words read in 60 seconds.
STRONG PASS	The student scores no more than 2 errors on the first pass through the passage and reads 102 or more words correct per minute. Proceed to Unit 4 or 5.
PASS	The student scores no more than 2 errors on the first pass through the passage and reads 81 to 101 words correct per minute. Proceed to Unit 4 or 5.
NO PASS	The student scores 3 or more errors on the first pass through the passage and/or reads 80 or fewer words correct per minute. Provide added fluency practice with *RW2* Unit 3 Extra Practice. (Lessons follow the certificate at the end of the teacher's guide.) After completing the Extra Practice, retest the student.

TRICKY WORD and FOCUS SKILL WARM-UP

| would | work | know | communities | guard | useful |

ORAL READING FLUENCY PASSAGE

Ant Colonies

★Did you know that ants live and work together? Just 10
like people, these amazing animals live and work together in 20
communities. 21

Think about it. If you were an ant, you would be very 33
useful. You would have an important job. You might guard the 44
nest or take care of the baby ants. You might be a cleanup worker 58
or gather food. Ants are very strong. If you were an ant, you 71
would drag big chunks of food back to the nest. 81

You might even grow up to be a queen. If you were the 94
queen, you would have your own room. You would lay thousands 105
and thousands of eggs. You would have a wonderful life. All the 117
other ants would wait on you! If you were an ant, what job would 131
you want? 133

SCORING Write student's name and date, mark any errors, and record total passage errors and WCPM on this page.

ORAL READING FLUENCY Start timing at the ★. Mark errors. Make a single slash in the text (/) at 60 seconds. Have the student complete the passage. If the student completes the passage in less than 60 seconds, have the student go back to the ★ and continue reading. Make a double slash (//) in the text at 60 seconds.

WCPM Determine words correct per minute by subtracting errors from words read in 60 seconds.

STRONG PASS The student scores no more than 2 errors on the first pass through the passage and reads 103 or more words correct per minute. Proceed to Unit 6.

PASS The student scores no more than 2 errors on the first pass through the passage and reads 82 to 102 words correct per minute. Proceed to Unit 6.

NO PASS The student scores 3 or more errors on the first pass through the passage and/or reads 81 or fewer words correct per minute. Provide added fluency practice with *RW2* Unit 5 Extra Practice. (Lessons follow the certificate at the end of the teacher's guide.) After completing the Extra Practice, retest the student.

TRICKY WORD and FOCUS SKILL WARM-UP

| alone | through | quite | commotion | which | congratulations |

ORAL READING FLUENCY PASSAGE

The Little Brown Puppy

★Dad and I walked to the pet store on Saturday. We liked   12
to watch the puppies through the window.   19

The clerk saw us and asked, "Would you like to hold a   31
puppy?"   32

I nodded my head, so the clerk reached into the cage to   44
pick up a puppy. There was quite a commotion. The puppies   55
started barking and jumping up and down. One little brown   65
puppy sat alone in a corner. The clerk asked, "Which puppy   76
would you like to hold?"   81

I said, "I'd like to hold that little brown puppy." The clerk   93
gave the puppy to me. It chewed on my finger and wagged its   106
tail. I smiled and said, "If we keep her, we could call her Fudge." 120

When Dad smiled, I knew we would get to take her home.   132
The clerk said, "Congratulations!"   136

SCORING	Write student's name and date, mark any errors, and record total passage errors and WCPM on this page.
ORAL READING FLUENCY	Start timing at the ★. Mark errors. Make a single slash in the text (/) at 60 seconds. Have the student complete the passage. If the student completes the passage in less than 60 seconds, have the student go back to the ★ and continue reading. Make a double slash in the text (//) at 60 seconds.
WCPM	Determine words correct per minute by subtracting errors from words read in 60 seconds.
STRONG PASS	The student scores no more than 2 errors on the first pass through the passage and reads 104 or more words correct per minute. Proceed to Unit 7.
PASS	The student scores no more than 2 errors on the first pass through the passage and reads 84 to 103 words correct per minute. Proceed to Unit 7.
NO PASS	The student scores 3 or more errors on the first pass through the passage and/or reads 83 or fewer words correct per minute. Provide added fluency practice with *RW2* Unit 6 Extra Practice. (Lessons follow the certificate at the end of the teacher's guide.) After completing the Extra Practice, retest the student.

TRICKY WORD and FOCUS SKILL WARM-UP

Hawaii	pencil	thought	snorkel	squawked	adventure

ORAL READING FLUENCY PASSAGE

To Hawaii and Back Home

★Miss Tam had a great time in Hawaii. She learned to   11
dance and snorkel. She visited a volcano and the rain forest. She   23
went many places and made new friends.   30

Going home was bittersweet. Miss Tam was sad to leave   40
her new friends, but she was happy to be going home.   51

When Miss Tam got home, Minnie Bird squawked,   59
"Hello." Then Old Scraggly Cat jumped into Miss Tam's arms.   69
Miss Tam said, "Oh, how nice to be at home!" She had a big   83
smile on her face.   87

For dinner, Miss Tam had red beans and rice. The next   98
day, she got on the city bus. She went to the library to see her   113
friends. She told them all about Hawaii. They thought the party   124
in the garage was strange. Everyone was excited to hear about   135
Miss Tam's adventure.   138

SCORING	Write student's name and date, mark any errors, and record total passage errors and WCPM on this page.
ORAL READING FLUENCY	Start timing at the ★. Mark errors. Make a single slash in the text (/) at 60 seconds. Have the student complete the passage. If the student completes the passage in less than 60 seconds, have the student go back to the ★ and continue reading. Make a double slash (//) in the text at 60 seconds.
WCPM	Determine words correct per minute by subtracting errors from words read in 60 seconds.
STRONG PASS	The student scores no more than 2 errors on the first pass through the passage and reads 106 or more words correct per minute. Proceed to Unit 8.
PASS	The student scores no more than 2 errors on the first pass through the passage and reads 85 to 105 words correct per minute. Proceed to Unit 8.
NO PASS	The student scores 3 or more errors on the first pass through the passage and/or reads 84 or fewer words correct per minute. Provide added fluency practice with RW2 Unit 7 Extra Practice. (Lessons follow the certificate at the end of the teacher's guide.) After completing the Extra Practice, retest the student.

TRICKY WORD and FOCUS SKILL WARM-UP

know	Ralph	delicious	phone	taught	curious

ORAL READING FLUENCY PASSAGE

Phillip's Soup

★ It was a cold winter day. We were hungry. "What   10
should we make for dinner?" asked Mom.   17

Phillip said, "I know how to make stone soup. Our   27
teacher taught us how to make it."   34

Mom heated a pot of water. Phillip chopped onions, and   44
Dad threw in some carrots. Then we decided to add some ham, 56
corn, and rice.   59

The soup began to smell so good that we decided to share   71
it with our friends. Mom went to the phone and invited some of 84
them to dinner. They were curious about the soup.   93

Soon everyone but Ralph had gathered at our house.   102
When the phone rang, Ralph said he would be here soon.   113

We waited and waited. When Ralph finally arrived, we   122
were all very hungry. The soup was delicious. We ate, laughed, 133
and had a great time together.   139

SCORING	Write student's name and date, mark any errors, and record total passage errors and WCPM on this page.
ORAL READING FLUENCY	Start timing at the ★. Mark errors. Make a single slash in the text (/) at 60 seconds. If the student completes the passage in less than 60 seconds, have the student go back to the ★ and continue reading. Make a double slash (//) in the text at 60 seconds.
WCPM	Determine words correct per minute by subtracting errors from words read in 60 seconds.
STRONG PASS	The student scores no more than 2 errors on the first pass through the passage and reads 107 or more words correct per minute. Proceed to Unit 9.
PASS	The student scores no more than 2 errors on the first pass through the passage and reads 86 to 106 words correct per minute. Proceed to Unit 9.
NO PASS	The student scores 3 or more errors on the first pass through the passage and/or reads 85 or fewer words correct per minute. Provide added fluency practice with *RW2* Unit 8 Extra Practice. (Lessons and BLMs follow the certificate at the end of the teacher's guide.) After completing the Extra Practice, retest the student.

| buy | ordinary | vegetables | knife | watch | bought |

A Cat Named Woody

☆Tess lived in a small village in Mexico. Every Saturday,　　10
there was an outdoor market in the center of town. Local farmers　　22
would bring fruits and vegetables to sell. There were tables piled　　33
high with sweet cakes for sale. You could buy flowers too. Tess　　45
and her mom went to the market every week.　　54

Phillip sold things at the market. He could turn ordinary　　64
wood into cats, dogs, cars, or trucks. Tess liked to watch him　　76
carve the wood with his sharp knife. Then he painted them in　　88
bright colors.　　90

Tess asked her mom for permission to buy a wood cat.　　101
She bought one with a long tail and huge paws. It had big green　　115
eyes. Phillip had painted the cat bright blue and yellow.　　125

"What will you call the cat?" asked Phillip.　　133

"His name is Woody!" said Tess.　　139

SCORING	Write student's name and date, mark any errors, and record total passage errors and WCPM on this page.
ORAL READING FLUENCY	Start timing at the ☆. Mark errors. Make a single slash in the text (/) at 60 seconds. If the student completes the passage in less than 60 seconds, have the student go back to the ☆ and continue reading. Make a double slash (//) in the text at 60 seconds.
WCPM	Determine words correct per minute by subtracting errors from words read in 60 seconds.
STRONG PASS	The student scores no more than 2 errors on the first pass through the passage and reads 109 or more words correct per minute. Proceed to Unit 10.
PASS	The student scores no more than 2 errors on the first pass through the passage and reads 87 to 108 words correct per minute. Proceed to Unit 10.
NO PASS	The student scores 3 or more errors on the first pass through the passage and/or reads 86 or fewer words correct per minute. Consider regrouping or a Jell-Well Review.

TRICKY WORD and FOCUS SKILL WARM-UP

soap	watched	whole	read	picture	front

ORAL READING FLUENCY PASSAGE

A Dream of Dinosaurs

⭐Ralph was a curious little boy. He wanted to know   10
about everything.   12

    "Why are there stars in the sky?" Ralph asked his mother.   23
Ralph's mother bought him a book about stars. Ralph read the   34
whole book from front to back.   40

    Ralph asked his father, "How does a computer work?"   49
Ralph's father took him to a lab. A scientist explained how the   61
computers work.   63

    "Why does soap float?" Ralph asked his sister. His sister   73
said, "Don't ask me! Go ask Grandpa." Grandpa helped Ralph   83
learn about soap on the computer.   89

    Ralph wanted to know about dinosaurs too. He read   98
many books about them. He watched some shows on TV about   109
dinosaurs. Then Ralph decided to write his own book. He wrote   120
down all he knew about dinosaurs. He drew pictures of them. He   132
showed his family the book. Everyone was impressed.   140

SCORING	Write student's name and date, mark any errors, and record total passage errors and WCPM on this page.
ORAL READING FLUENCY	Start timing at the ⭐. Mark errors. Make a single slash in the text (/) at 60 seconds. Have the student complete the passage. If the student completes the passage in less than 60 seconds, have the student go back to the ⭐ and continue reading. Make a double slash (//) in the text at 60 seconds.
WCPM	Determine words correct per minute by subtracting errors from words read in 60 seconds.
STRONG PASS	The student scores no more than 2 errors on the first pass through the passage and reads 110 or more words correct per minute. Proceed to Unit 11.
PASS	The student scores no more than 2 errors on the first pass through the passage and reads 88 to 109 words correct per minute. Proceed to Unit 11.
NO PASS	The student scores 3 or more errors on the first pass through the passage and/or reads 87 or fewer words correct per minute. Provide added fluency practice with *RW2* Unit 10 Extra Practice. (Lessons follow the certificate at the end of the teacher's guide.) After completing the Extra Practice, retest the student.

TRICKY WORD and FOCUS SKILL WARM-UP

point	breakfast	Howie	believe	climb	entrance

ORAL READING FLUENCY PASSAGE

The Amazing Dinosaur

★My brother Howie and I were excited. Mom was taking   10

us to the big museum to see the dinosaur fossils. First, she made   23

us eat breakfast. Then we put on our coats and walked to the   36

train station. We all climbed on the train for the long trip into the   50

city.   51

Finally, Mom said, "We're here!" We jumped off the   60

train. Mom knew the way to the museum. When we saw the   72

museum, Howie and I could hardly believe our eyes. It was   83

huge!   84

We hopped up the steps and walked through the front   94

doors. Howie gave me a nudge and pointed. "Look, Sue's over   105

there!" An enormous skeleton of an extinct T. rex stood near the   117

entrance. Howie and I ran over to look at it. We felt as small as   132

ants next to Sue. It was really amazing!   140

SCORING	Write student's name and date, mark any errors, and record total passage errors and WCPM on this page.
ORAL READING FLUENCY	Start timing at the ★. Mark errors. Make a single slash in the text (/) at 60 seconds. Have the student complete the passage. If the student completes the passage in less than 60 seconds, have the student go back to the ★ and continue reading. Make a double slash in the text (//) at 60 seconds.
WCPM	Determine words correct per minute by subtracting errors from words read in 60 seconds.
STRONG PASS	The student scores no more than 2 errors on the first pass through the passage and reads 111 or more words correct per minute. Proceed to Unit 12.
PASS	The student scores no more than 2 errors on the first pass through the passage and reads 89 to 110 words correct per minute. Proceed to Unit 12.
NO PASS	The student scores 3 or more errors on the first pass through the passage and/or reads 88 or fewer words correct per minute. Provide added fluency practice with *RW2* Unit 11 Extra Practice. (Lessons follow the certificate at the end of the teacher's guide.) After completing the Extra Practice, retest the student.

TRICKY WORD and FOCUS SKILL WARM-UP

imagine	ancient	choice	reptile	laughed	above

ORAL READING FLUENCY PASSAGE

A Pretend Pteranodon

⭐Cole read lots of books. He loved to study ancient   10
reptiles and dinosaurs. He liked to imagine what it would be like   22
to meet one.   25

    "If you could meet an ancient creature, which one would   35
you choose?" Cole asked everyone he saw.   42

    Cole knew what his choice would be. He really wanted to   53
meet a Pteranodon. He could almost see one soaring high above   64
the treetops. He could imagine hearing its loud, screeching call.   74

    "Look at those giant wings," Cole said as he pointed to the 86
large picture in his book. "I want to ride on a Pteranodon."   98

    "Let's pretend, Cole," said Lilly. Cole's sister loved to 107
pretend. She scrambled onto the bed, spread her arms wide, and   118
jumped.   119

    "Look, Cole. I'm flying!" shouted Lilly as she flapped her 129
arms.   130

    Cole laughed. Then he sighed and turned back to his   140
dinosaur book.   142

SCORING	Write student's name and date, mark any errors, and record total passage errors and WCPM on this page.
ORAL READING FLUENCY	Start timing at the ⭐. Mark errors. Make a single slash in the text (/) at 60 seconds. If the student completes the passage in less than 60 seconds, have the student go back to the ⭐ and continue reading. Make a double slash (//) in the text at 60 seconds.
WCPM	Determine words correct per minute by subtracting errors from words read in 60 seconds.
STRONG PASS	The student scores no more than 2 errors on the first pass through the passage and reads 112 or more words correct per minute. Continue with Unit 12.
PASS	The student scores no more than 2 errors on the first pass through the passage and reads 91 to 111 words correct per minute. Continue with Unit 12.
NO PASS	The student scores 3 or more errors on the first pass through the passage and/or reads 90 or fewer words correct per minute. Provide added fluency practice with Chapters 1–5, *Dinosaurs Before Dark*.

TRICKY WORD and FOCUS SKILL WARM-UP

imagine	heard	straight	toward	reptile	valley

ORAL READING FLUENCY PASSAGE

Franny and Paul

⭐What would Pteranodons say if they could talk? Let's   9
imagine.   10

"How are your babies, Franny?" asked Paul. The two   19
reptiles were soaring through the air. They glanced down at the 30
nests in the valley.   34

"My babies are growing. I am bringing them plants to   44
eat," said Franny proudly. Franny shouted to her babies, "I'm   54
coming! Food's on the way!"   59

Franny pointed her head toward the nest. Paul said, "Soon   69
they will be ready to get their own food."   78

Paul spread his giant wings again. He started to fly   88
away when he saw a horrible sight. A stampede! Hundreds of   99
dinosaurs were scrambling through the valley. They were in   108
a panic.   Paul heard a loud roar. It was Rex, the meat-eating 121
dinosaur everyone feared.   124

"Hurry home!" said Paul to Franny. "Rex is hunting!"   133
Franny nodded and flew straight down to her nest.   142

SCORING	Write student's name and date, mark any errors, and record total passage errors and WCPM on this page.
ORAL READING FLUENCY	Start timing at the ⭐. Mark errors. Make a single slash in the text (/) at 60 seconds. Have the student complete the passage. If the student completes the passage in less than 60 seconds, have the student go back to the ⭐ and continue reading. Make a double slash in the text (//) at 60 seconds.
WCPM	Determine words correct per minute by subtracting errors from words read in 60 seconds.
STRONG PASS	The student scores no more than 2 errors on the first pass through the passage and reads 112 or more words correct per minute. Proceed to Unit 13.
PASS	The student scores no more than 2 errors on the first pass through the passage and reads 91 to 111 words correct per minute. Proceed to Unit 13.
NO PASS	The student scores 3 or more errors on the first pass through the passage and/or reads 90 or fewer words correct per minute. Provide added fluency practice with *RW2* Unit 12 Extra Practice. (Lessons follow the certificate at the end of the teacher's guide.) After completing the Extra Practice, retest the student.

TRICKY WORD and FOCUS SKILL WARM-UP

screeched	watched	sparkled	Grandfather	climbed

ORAL READING FLUENCY PASSAGE

Gray Cloud and Grandfather

★It was going to be an amazing day. Gray Cloud could   11

see the sun peeking over the mountains. Shadow and light filled   22

the clearing where Grandfather's wigwam stood. Birds began to   31

sing in the great pine trees at the edge of the meadow. Dewdrops   44

sparkled on the tall green grass.   50

Gray Cloud put one knee down on the ground and   60

watched a spider spin its web. As the sun slowly climbed higher   72

in the sky, the buzzing sound of insects grew louder and louder.   84

A raven screeched. Gray Cloud looked up.   91

Grandfather stood beside him. "You are a good boy, Gray   101

Cloud. You see with both eyes at once, and you listen with both   114

ears at once."   117

Gray Cloud smiled and jumped to his feet. It was a   128

perfect day for a long hike. He and Grandfather started walking   139

down the sunny trail.   143

SCORING	Write student's name and date, mark any errors, and record total passage errors and WCPM on this page.
ORAL READING FLUENCY	Start timing at the ★. Mark errors. Make a single slash in the text (/) at 60 seconds. Have the student complete the passage. If the student completes the passage in less than 60 seconds, have the student go back to the ★ and continue reading. Make a double slash (//) in the text at 60 seconds.
WCPM	Determine words correct per minute by subtracting errors from words read in 60 seconds.
STRONG PASS	The student scores no more than 2 errors on the first pass through the passage and reads 114 or more words correct per minute. Proceed to Unit 14.
PASS	The student scores no more than 2 errors on the first pass through the passage and reads 93 to 113 words correct per minute. Proceed to Unit 14.
NO PASS	The student scores 3 or more errors on the first pass through the passage and/or reads 92 or fewer words correct per minute. Provide added fluency practice with *RW2* Unit 13 Extra Practice. (Lessons follow the certificate at the end of the teacher's guide.) After completing the Extra Practice, retest the student.

TRICKY WORD and FOCUS SKILL WARM-UP

wondered	warmer	fruit	roosted	stomach	curious

ORAL READING FLUENCY PASSAGE

The Curious Bat

★Bob was a curious brown bat. The other bats in his   11

colony ate bugs, but Bob wondered what fruit tasted like. He   22

tried to eat an apple. It got stuck in his sharp teeth, and his   36

stomach hurt. Bob decided bugs were best.   43

The other bats roosted in the cave. Bob wondered what   53

it would be like to fly in the sunshine. Bob could hardly keep his   67

eyes open in the bright sun. He tried to find a nice moth to eat,   82

but they all hid from him. Bob decided the dark night was better   95

than a sunny day.   99

The other bats flew to a warmer place for the winter. Bob   111

wondered what winter was like. When it finally snowed, he   121

thought, "I'm very cold, and I miss my friends." So off he flew to   135

join the other bats in their new warm cave.   144

SCORING	Write student's name and date, mark any errors, and record total passage errors and WCPM on this page.
ORAL READING FLUENCY	Start timing at the ★ Mark errors. Make a single slash in the text (/) at 60 seconds. Have the student complete the passage. If the student completes the passage in less than 60 seconds, have the student go back to the ★ and continue reading. Make a double slash (//) in the text at 60 seconds.
WCPM	Determine words correct per minute by subtracting errors from words read in 60 seconds.
STRONG PASS	The student scores no more than 2 errors on the first pass through the passage and reads 115 or more words correct per minute. Proceed to Unit 15.
PASS	The student scores no more than 2 errors on the first pass through the passage and reads 94 to 114 words correct per minute. Proceed to Unit 15.
NO PASS	The student scores 3 or more errors on the first pass through the passage and/or reads 93 or fewer words correct per minute. Provide added fluency practice with *RW2* Unit 14 Extra Practice. (Lessons follow the certificate at the end of the teacher's guide.) After completing the Extra Practice, retest the student.

TRICKY WORD and FOCUS SKILL WARM-UP

covered	thought	buffalo	Roy	dangerous	traveled

ORAL READING FLUENCY PASSAGE

Imagine the Wild West

★Roy enjoyed reading books about the Wild West. He 　　　9
thought it would be fun to live during those times. He thought 　　21
that being a settler moving to the West would be cool. 　　32

"Riding in a covered wagon would be fun," he told his 　　43
mother. "I could play in the back of the wagon. I might see 　　56
buffalo, snakes, and wolves too." 　　61

"It may sound cool, but life was hard," said his mother. 　　72
"Sometimes the dangerous trip took months. Often, people had 　　81
to walk behind the wagons. They traveled in the bitter cold and 　　93
in blazing heat. There were no beds to sleep in, and there were 　　106
no cars to ride in." 　　111

"I think it might be fun for a while but not for a long 　　125
time," said Roy. "I still like reading about the Wild West, but 　　137
having a bed and car is a real joy." 　　146

SCORING	Write student's name and date, mark any errors, and record total passage errors and WCPM on this page.
ORAL READING FLUENCY	Start timing at the ★. Mark errors. Make a single slash in the text (/) at 60 seconds. If the student completes the passage in less than 60 seconds, have the student go back to the ★ and continue reading. Make a double slash (//) in the text at 60 seconds.
WCPM	Determine words correct per minute by subtracting errors from words read in 60 seconds.
STRONG PASS	The student scores no more than 2 errors on the first pass through the passage and reads 116 or more words correct per minute. Proceed to Unit 16.
PASS	The student scores no more than 2 errors on the first pass through the passage and reads 95 to 115 words correct per minute. Proceed to Unit 16.
NO PASS	The student scores 3 or more errors on the first pass through the passage and/or reads 94 or fewer words correct per minute. Provide added fluency practice with *RW2* Unit 15 Extra Practice. (Lessons follow the certificate at the end of the teacher's guide.) After completing the Extra Practice, retest the student.

TRICKY WORD and FOCUS SKILL WARM-UP

| powerful | Firecracker | blizzard | suddenly | jacket |

ORAL READING FLUENCY PASSAGE

My Horse, Firecracker

★Cold, white, wet snow was all around. All I could see — 11
was my horse's thick black mane in front of me. I could feel — 24
his powerful legs working hard as he walked slowly through the — 35
snow. I tucked my face down into my jacket and pulled my hat — 48
on tight. — 50

The blizzard had surprised us. We were rounding up — 59
cattle when the storm came up suddenly. Now all I wanted was — 71
to get back to the camp. The other cowboys would be looking for — 84
us. The cook would have a warm fire and hot food for me. He — 98
would have a blanket and oats for Firecracker. — 106

"Hurry, take us home, Firecracker," I said. Firecracker — 114
snorted. His ears went back and forth when I spoke. I was lost, — 127
but my horse knew the way home. I trusted him to take us back — 141
safely through the dangerous blizzard. — 146

SCORING Write student's name and date, mark any errors, and record total passage errors and WCPM on this page.

ORAL READING FLUENCY Start timing at the ★. Mark errors. Make a single slash in the text (/) at 60 seconds. Have the student complete the passage. If the student completes the passage in less than 60 seconds, have the student go back to the ★ and continue reading. Make a double slash (//) in the text at 60 seconds.

WCPM Determine words correct per minute by subtracting errors from words read in 60 seconds.

STRONG PASS The student scores no more than 2 errors on the first pass through the passage and reads 118 or more words correct per minute. Proceed to Unit 17.

PASS The student scores no more than 2 errors on the first pass through the passage and reads 97 to 117 words correct per minute. Proceed to Unit 17.

NO PASS The student scores 3 or more errors on the first pass through the passage and/or reads 96 or fewer words correct per minute. Provide added fluency practice with RW2 Unit 16 Extra Practice. (Lessons follow the certificate at the end of the teacher's guide.) After completing the Extra Practice, retest the student.

TRICKY WORD and FOCUS SKILL WARM-UP

predators	prey	listened	zebra	watched	western

ORAL READING FLUENCY PASSAGE

At the Water Hole

⭐The day was coming to an end. The hot sun was finally   12
setting in the western sky. All day long, the zebra herd grazed on   25
dry grass. The lion pride spent the day sleeping in the shade of a   39
big tree. Now all the animals needed to drink.   48

      The lions stood up slowly, one by one, and began walking   59
to the water hole. Their giant paws made no sound on the dusty   72
ground. They were predators, at the top of the food chain. They   84
had nothing to fear.   88

      The zebras also walked slowly to the water hole. They   98
were prey animals. They watched and listened for predators.   107
They were ready to run if there was danger.   116

      The zebras and lions came together at the water hole. The   127
lions were not hungry. They would hunt tomorrow. The zebras   137
were safe. They all took turns drinking the cool, clear water.   148

SCORING	Write student's name and date, mark any errors, and record total passage errors and WCPM on this page.
ORAL READING FLUENCY	Start timing at the ⭐. Mark errors. Make a single slash in the text (/) at 60 seconds. Have the student complete the passage. If the student completes the passage in less than 60 seconds, have the student go back to the ⭐ and continue reading. Make a double slash (//) in the text at 60 seconds.
WCPM	Determine words correct per minute by subtracting errors from words read in 60 seconds.
STRONG PASS	The student scores no more than 2 errors on the first pass through the passage and reads 119 or more words correct per minute. Proceed to Unit 18.
PASS	The student scores no more than 2 errors on the first pass through the passage and reads 98 to 118 words correct per minute. Proceed to Unit 18.
NO PASS	The student scores 3 or more errors on the first pass through the passage and/or reads 97 or fewer words correct per minute. Provide added fluency practice with *RW2* Unit 17 Extra Practice. (Lessons follow the certificate at the end of the teacher's guide.) After completing the Extra Practice, retest the student.

TRICKY WORD and FOCUS SKILL WARM-UP

chuckled	unusual	library	listened	slither	diving

ORAL READING FLUENCY PASSAGE

Miss Tam's Dream

★After a fun day diving in the sea, Miss Tam was reading   12
a book about the coral reef. She looked at the great pictures and   25
thought about her day. What an adventure! Then Miss Tam's   35
eyes began to close. She was very tired. Soon the book dropped   47
to the floor. Miss Tam was sound asleep.   55

Miss Tam was back at the library reading a story. A giant   67
clam, an orange and white clownfish, and a green sea turtle sat   79
next to her. A huge eel kept sliding off his chair. Then he would   93
slither back onto it. All the animals listened carefully to Miss   104
Tam's story.   106

When Miss Tam finished the story, they all had rice and   117
beans with ice cream. "My, this is unusual," thought Miss Tam.   128
"We're eating snacks in the library."   134

Suddenly Miss Tam opened her eyes. Then she chuckled.   143
"What a dream!" she said.   148

SCORING	Write student's name and date, mark any errors, and record total passage errors and WCPM on this page.
ORAL READING FLUENCY	Start timing at the ★. Mark errors. Make a single slash in the text (/) at 60 seconds. If the student completes the passage in less than 60 seconds, have the student go back to the ★ and continue reading. Make a double slash (//) in the text at 60 seconds.
WCPM	Determine words correct per minute by subtracting errors from words read in 60 seconds.
STRONG PASS	The student scores no more than 2 errors on the first pass through the passage and reads 120 or more words correct per minute. Proceed to Unit 19.
PASS	The student scores no more than 2 errors on the first pass through the passage and reads 99 to 119 words correct per minute. Proceed to Unit 19.
NO PASS	The student scores 3 or more errors on the first pass through the passage and/or reads 98 or fewer words correct per minute. Provide added fluency practice with *RW2* Unit 18 Extra Practice. (Lessons follow the certificate at the end of the teacher's guide.) After completing the Extra Practice, retest the student.

TRICKY WORD and FOCUS SKILL WARM-UP

| vacation | bulletin | seashore | clothes | polite | cheerfully |

ORAL READING FLUENCY PASSAGE

The Yard Sale

★Brandon and Robert decided to have a yard sale. They   10
wanted to earn some money for a trip to the seashore.   21

Mrs. Wilson thought the sale was a great idea. She gave   32
the boys a couch, a bulletin board, and some picture frames.   43
Brandon found some old clothes in his room that were too small   55
for him.   57

The boys made a sign that said "yard sale" in big letters.   69
They cut the grass and cleaned up the yard. They set up some   82
tables. Then they put out all the things they wanted to sell.   94

The brothers were very polite to the people who came to   105
their sale. "Two dollars, please" and "thank you very much!"   115
they said cheerfully. Soon everything was gone, except for the 125
bulletin board. It was so big and heavy that no one wanted it. 138
Robert thought he would hang it on the wall above his bed.   150

SCORING	Write student's name and date, mark any errors, and record total passage errors and WCPM on this page.
ORAL READING FLUENCY	Start timing at the ★. Mark errors. Make a single slash in the text (/) at 60 seconds. If the student completes the passage in less than 60 seconds, have the student go back to the ★ and continue reading. Make a double slash (//) in the text at 60 seconds.
WCPM	Determine words correct per minute by subtracting errors from words read in 60 seconds.
STRONG PASS	The student scores no more than 2 errors on the first pass through the passage and reads 122 or more words correct per minute. Proceed to Unit 20.
PASS	The student scores no more than 2 errors on the first pass through the passage and reads 101 to 121 words correct per minute. Proceed to Unit 20.
NO PASS	The student scores 3 or more errors on the first pass through the passage and/or reads 100 or fewer words correct per minute. Provide added fluency practice with *RW2* Unit 19 Extra Practice. (Lessons follow the certificate at the end of the teacher's guide.) After the student completes the Extra Practice, retest the student.

TRICKY WORD and FOCUS SKILL WARM-UP

| stomach | microscope | gurgling | disgusting | unbelievable | examine |

ORAL READING FLUENCY PASSAGE

The Best Day of My Life

★Some day I'm going to be a doctor. For me, science   11

class is always exciting. Last week we studied the human body.   22

Our teacher had us learn about the stomach first. We watched   33

a film and heard a gurgling stomach. We saw chunks of food   45

that the stomach was churning and mashing around. It looked   55

disgusting and very cool!   59

Next, we looked at giant red blood cells under a   69

microscope. The cells jumped and bounced around like big red   79

balls. Our teacher said that blood cells go on a wild ride through   92

the heart, lungs, and brain.   97

The most unbelievable thing happened last Friday. A   105

doctor came to our class and brought a real pig's heart for us   118

to examine. It was fascinating. Someone told me later that the   129

whole class turned green. Everyone but me. I got to hold the   141

heart, but nobody else did. That was the best day of my life!   154

SCORING	Write student's name and date, mark any errors, and record total passage errors and WCPM on this page.
ORAL READING FLUENCY	Start timing at the ★. Mark errors. Make a single slash in the text (/) at 60 seconds. If the student completes the passage in less than 60 seconds, have the student go back to the ★ and continue reading. Make a double slash (//) in the text at 60 seconds.
WCPM	Determine words correct per minute by subtracting errors from words read in 60 seconds.
STRONG PASS	The student scores no more than 2 errors on the first pass through the passage and reads 123 or more words correct per minute. Proceed to Unit 21.
PASS	The student scores no more than 2 errors on the first pass through the passage and reads 102 to 122 words correct per minute. Proceed to Unit 21.
NO PASS	The student scores 3 or more errors on the first pass through the passage and/or reads 101 or fewer words correct per minute. Provide added decoding and fluency practice. For 2 or 3 days, reteach an exercise page and use a homework passage for fluency practice, then retest.

TRICKY WORD and FOCUS SKILL WARM-UP

borrow	expensive	inspired	neighbor	terrible

ORAL READING FLUENCY PASSAGE

Abe Borrows a Book

★Abraham Lincoln loved to read. One day he heard that   10
a neighbor had a new book. It was called *The Life of George*   23
Washington. Abe walked many miles to borrow the book. The   33
book was expensive, so he promised to return it in good shape. 45

George Washington's life story inspired Lincoln.   51
Washington was a farmer too, and he became the first president 62
of the United States. As Abe read the book, perhaps he thought 74
about becoming president.   77

One night Abe left the book too close to the fire. In the   90
morning the book's cover was burned. Lincoln felt terrible. He 100
would have to tell his friend the truth. He walked back to his 113
friend's farm.   115

Abraham didn't have any money, so he offered to work to   126
pay for the book. He worked on the farm for three days. But at the 141
end of the three days, his friend gave him the book to keep!   154

SCORING	Write student's name and date, mark any errors, and record total passage errors and WCPM on this page.
ORAL READING FLUENCY	Start timing at the ★. Mark errors. Make a single slash in the text (/) at 60 seconds. If the student completes the passage in less than 60 seconds, have the student go back to the ★and continue reading. Make a double slash (//) in the text at 60 seconds.
WCPM	Determine words correct per minute by subtracting errors from words read in 60 seconds.
STRONG PASS	The student scores no more than 2 errors on the first pass through the passage and reads 125 or more words correct per minute. Proceed to Unit 22.
PASS	The student scores no more than 2 errors on the first pass through the passage and reads 104 to 124 words correct per minute. Proceed to Unit 22.
NO PASS	The student scores 3 or more errors on the first pass through the passage and/or reads 103 or fewer words correct per minute. Provide added fluency practice. For 2 or 3 days, reteach an exercise page and use a homework passage for fluency practice, then retest.

| success | invention | machine | phonograph | idea |

ORAL READING FLUENCY PASSAGE

Edison's Ideas

★Thomas Edison had many great ideas, and he worked   9

hard. Even so, not all of his ideas became great inventions.   20

Edison invented a machine that played sound. He   28

also built a machine that made pictures move. He put the two   40

machines together and made the first talking movie. It was hard   51

to keep the sound and the picture going at the same time. A   64

man's mouth would move, but you couldn't hear his voice until a   76

few seconds later! This machine was not a success.   85

Edison also made a doll that talked. He put a small   96

phonograph inside the doll. When a handle was turned, the doll   107

would tell a short story. The dolls worked fine in Edison's shop,   119

but they didn't work in the stores. They all broke on the way to   133

the stores! The talking doll was not a success. That didn't stop   145

Tom Edison. He just moved on to his next great idea.   156

SCORING	Write student's name and date, mark any errors, and record total passage errors and WCPM on this page.
ORAL READING FLUENCY	Start timing at the ★. Mark errors. Make a single slash in the text (/) at 60 seconds. Have the student complete the passage. If the student completes the passage in less than 60 seconds, have the student go back to the ★ and continue reading. Make a double slash (//) in the text at 60 seconds.
WCPM	Determine words correct per minute by subtracting errors from words read in 60 seconds.
STRONG PASS	The student scores no more than 2 errors on the first pass through the passage and reads 126 or more words correct per minute. Proceed to Unit 23.
PASS	The student scores no more than 2 errors on the first pass through the passage and reads 106 to 125 words correct per minute. Proceed to Unit 23.
NO PASS	The student scores 3 or more errors on the first pass through the passage and/or reads 105 or fewer words correct per minute. Provide added fluency practice. For 2 or 3 days, reteach an exercise page and use a homework passage for fluency practice, then retest.

TRICKY WORD and FOCUS SKILL WARM-UP

recognized	covered	scurried	enough	temperature	confused

ORAL READING FLUENCY PASSAGE

Toby and Flash

☆Toby and Flash were just a few weeks old. Their plump   11
bodies were covered with fluffy gray feathers. They were still   21
small enough to enjoy perching on their father's feet. But they   32
were also discovering that it was fun to explore.   41

One day Toby and Flash wandered off. They roamed the   51
vast land surrounding the penguin rookery. Then Toby began to   61
feel unsettled. He looked around. "Flash, I'm confused. Where   70
are we?" he said. "I'm hungry, and freezing cold! Let's find our   82
parents."   83

Flash hesitated. The temperature was dropping. He   90
didn't want to admit it, but he was freezing too. "Ok, Toby, if you   104
insist. We'll go back." Flash turned around and began to strut   115
back to the penguin colony. Toby scurried after him.   124

Then, in the distance, two emperor penguins emerged   132
from the huddled group and bellowed. Flash and Toby   141
recognized them. They were thrilled. They ran as fast as they   152
could to their fathers.   156

SCORING	Write student's name and date, mark any errors, and record total passage errors and WCPM on this page.
ORAL READING FLUENCY	Start timing at the ☆. Mark errors. Make a single slash in the text (/) at 60 seconds. If the student completes the passage in less than 60 seconds, have the student go back to the ☆ and continue reading. Make a double slash (//) in the text at 60 seconds.
WCPM	Determine words correct per minute by subtracting errors from words read in 60 seconds.
STRONG PASS	The student scores no more than 2 errors on the first pass through the passage and reads 128 or more words correct per minute. Proceed to Unit 24.
PASS	The student scores no more than 2 errors on the first pass through the passage and reads 107 to 127 words correct per minute. Proceed to Unit 24.
NO PASS	The student scores 3 or more errors on the first pass through the passage and/or reads 106 or fewer words correct per minute. Provide added fluency practice. For 2 or 3 days, reteach an exercise page and use a homework passage for fluency practice, then retest.

TRICKY WORD and FOCUS SKILL WARM-UP

ecosystem	endangered	recycle	heroine	determined

ORAL READING FLUENCY PASSAGE

A Rain Forest Heroine

⭐Jane is in the second grade. She wrote a report about   11
the rain forest. She entered the report in a contest. Jane didn't   23
think she would win, but she did! The prize was a trip to the rain   38
forest. She went on the trip with her parents.   47

Jane got to see an ecosystem that is very different from the   59
forest near her home. She thought the rain forest was beautiful.   70
She went hiking and swimming. She went on a boat trip down a   83
river. She saw many endangered plants and animals.   91

When Jane returned home, she wanted to do even more   101
to help heal the Earth. She helped her family and friends recycle. 113
She did the same thing at school. She raised money to buy land   126
in the rain forest.   130

Jane wants to be a scientist someday and help save the   141
animals and plants. She is determined to study hard and learn   152
everything she can about the rain forest.   159

SCORING	Write student's name and date, mark any errors, and record total passage errors and WCPM on this page.
ORAL READING FLUENCY	Start timing at the ⭐. Mark errors. Make a single slash in the text (/) at 60 seconds. Have the student complete the passage. If the student completes the passage in less than 60 seconds, have the student go back to the ⭐ and continue reading. Make a double slash (//) in the text at 60 seconds.
WCPM	Determine words correct per minute by subtracting errors from words read in 60 seconds.
STRONG PASS	The student scores no more than 2 errors on the first pass through the passage and reads 131 or more words correct per minute. Proceed to Unit 25.
PASS	The student scores no more than 2 errors on the first pass through the passage and reads 110 to 130 words correct per minute. Proceed to Unit 25.
NO PASS	The student scores 3 or more errors on the first pass through the passage and/or reads 109 or fewer words correct per minute. Provide added fluency practice. For 2 or 3 days, reteach an exercise page and use a homework passage for fluency practice, then retest.

TRICKY WORD and FOCUS SKILL WARM-UP

lose	glistening	peculiar	laughed	mischievous

ORAL READING FLUENCY PASSAGE

A Mystery

☆ "How peculiar. My watch has disappeared," said   7
Emma's mother. "I put it right here on the picnic table, and now   20
it's gone." Emma helped her search for the watch. They couldn't   31
locate it anywhere.   34

The next day, Emma put her shiny ring on the porch so   46
she wouldn't lose it while she was playing. When she came back,   58
it had disappeared. Emma and her mother rummaged around the   68
yard again.   70

Then Emma saw something glistening in the sun over by   80
the enormous oak tree. She quickly ran to the tree and discovered 92
the watch and the ring on the ground beneath it. But how did they 106
get way over by the big oak tree?   114

She looked up. A mischievous crow sat on a branch with   125
a shiny silver button in its beak! The bird winked at Emma,   137
gave a muffled squawk, and dropped the button. Emma's mother   147
laughed and said, "Oh my! I have heard that crows like to collect 160
shiny things. Mystery solved!"   164

SCORING	Write student's name and date, mark any errors, and record total passage errors and WCPM on this page.
ORAL READING FLUENCY	Start timing at the ☆. Mark errors. Make a single slash in the text (/) at 60 seconds. Have the student complete the passage. If the student completes the passage in less than 60 seconds, have the student go back to the ☆ and continue reading. Make a double slash (//) in the text at 60 seconds.
WCPM	Determine words correct per minute by subtracting errors from words read in 60 seconds.
STRONG PASS	The student scores no more than 2 errors on the first pass through the passage and reads 133 or more words correct per minute.
PASS	The student scores no more than 2 errors on the first pass through the passage and reads 112 to 132 words correct per minute.
	Assess for placement in a 3^2 (mid–third grade) or 4^1 (early fourth grade) reading program.

INSTRUCTOR: _____

Unit		A		B		C		D		E	
Assessment Date											
Goal Pass		WCPM 55	ERRORS 0–2	WCPM 60	ERRORS 0–2	WCPM 65	ERRORS 0–2	WCPM 70	ERRORS 0–2	WCPM 75	ERRORS 0–2
Acceleration		85		85		90		95		100	
1.											
2.											
3.											
4.											
5.											
6.											
7.											
8.											
9.											
10.											
11.											
12.											
13.											
14.											
15.											
Comments											

Fluency Foundations Group ORF Assessment Record

INSTRUCTOR: _____

Unit	F		G		H		I		J	
Assessment Date										
Goal **Pass**	WCPM 80	ERRORS 0–2	WCPM 82	ERRORS 0–2	WCPM 85	ERRORS 0–2	WCPM 88	ERRORS 0–2	WCPM 90	ERRORS 0–2
Acceleration	105		105		110		110		—	
1.										
2.										
3.										
4.										
5.										
6.										
7.										
8.										
9.										
10.										
11.										
12.										
13.										
14.										
15.										
Comments										

98   Blackline Master   ©2009 Sopris West Educational Services. All rights reserved.

NAME: _____

Oral Reading Fluency Assessments

Unit	Date	Pass	Acceleration	Accuracy Score	ORF Score (WCPM)	Comments
A		55+	85			
B		60+	85			
C		65+	90			
D		70+	95			
E		75+	100			
F		80+	105			
G		82+	105			
H		85+	110			
I		88+	110			
J		90+	—			

INSTRUCTOR: _____

Unit	1		2		3		4		5	
Assessment Date							Diagnostic as needed—no assessment			
Goal	WCPM	ERRORS	WCPM	ERRORS	WCPM	ERRORS	WCPM	ERRORS	WCPM	ERRORS
Pass	80	0–2	80	0–2	81	0–2			82	0–2
Strong Pass	101		101		102				103	
1.										
2.										
3.										
4.										
5.										
6.										
7.										
8.										
9.										
10.										
11.										
12.										
13.										
14.										
15.										
Comments										

INSTRUCTOR: _____

Unit	6		7		8		9		10	
Assessment Date										
Goal Pass	WCPM 84	ERRORS 0–2	WCPM 85	ERRORS 0–2	WCPM 86	ERRORS 0–2	WCPM 87	ERRORS 0–2	WCPM 88	ERRORS 0–2
Strong Pass	104		106		107		109		110	
1.										
2.										
3.										
4.										
5.										
6.										
7.										
8.										
9.										
10.										
11.										
12.										
13.										
14.										
15.										
Comments										

INSTRUCTOR: _____

Unit	11		12		13		14		15	
Assessment Date										
Goal Pass	WCPM 89	ERRORS 0–2	WCPM 91	ERRORS 0–2	WCPM 93	ERRORS 0–2	WCPM 94	ERRORS 0–2	WCPM 95	ERRORS 0–2
Strong Pass	111		112		114		115		116	
1.										
2.										
3.										
4.										
5.										
6.										
7.										
8.										
9.										
10.										
11.										
12.										
13.										
14.										
15.										
Comments										

INSTRUCTOR: _____

Unit	16		17		18		19		20	
Assessment Date										
Goal Pass	WCPM 97	ERRORS 0–2	WCPM 98	ERRORS 0–2	WCPM 99	ERRORS 0–2	WCPM 101	ERRORS 0–2	WCPM 102	ERRORS 0–2
Strong Pass	118		119		120		122		123	
1.										
2.										
3.										
4.										
5.										
6.										
7.										
8.										
9.										
10.										
11.										
12.										
13.										
14.										
15.										

Comments

INSTRUCTOR: _____

Unit	21		22		23		24		25	
Assessment Date										
Goal **Pass**	WCPM 104	ERRORS 0–2	WCPM 106	ERRORS 0–2	WCPM 107	ERRORS 0–2	WCPM 110	ERRORS 0–2	WCPM 112	ERRORS 0–2
Strong Pass	125		126		128		131		133	
1.										
2.										
3.										
4.										
5.										
6.										
7.										
8.										
9.										
10.										
11.										
12.										
13.										
14.										
15.										
Comments										

NAME: _____

Oral Reading Fluency Assessments

Unit	Date	Pass	Strong Pass	Accuracy Score	ORF Score (WCPM)	Comments
1		80–100	101+			
2		80–100	101+			
3		81–101	102+			
4		no assessment				
5		82–102	103+			
6		84–103	104+			
7		85–105	106+			
8		86–106	107+			
9		87–108	109+			
10		88–109	110+			
11		89–110	111+			
12 mid-unit		91–111	112+			
12		91–111	112+			
13		93–113	114+			
14		94–114	115+			
15		95–115	116+			
16		97–117	118+			
17		98–118	119+			
18		99–119	120+			
19		101–121	122+			
20		102–122	123+			
21		104–124	125+			
22		106–125	126+			
23		107–127	128+			
24		110–130	131+			
25		112–132	133+			

Individual Written Assessment Record (1 of 2)

	Date	Genre Readability	Item 1	Item 2	Item 3	Item 4	Item 5	Item 6	Items 7 and 8	Total
Unit 5		Fiction, Imaginative	Main Character	Goal	Problem	Inference	Solution	Vocabulary • impressed	Characterization, Written	
Unit 6		Fiction, Imaginative	Main Character, Narrator	Topic	Goal	Action	Vocabulary • exhausting	Drawing Conclusions	Characterization, Written	
Unit 7		Fiction, Imaginative	Main Character	Setting	Vocabulary • fascinated	Supporting Details	Main Idea	Main Idea Statement		
Unit 8		Fiction, Realistic	Main Character	Beginning	Middle	End	Vocabulary • bittersweet	Characterization		
Unit 9		Personal Narrative	Narrator	Main Idea	Vocabulary • tradition	Vocabulary • commotion	Sequence	Inference	End, Written	
Unit 10		Nonfiction	Topic	Main Idea	Vocabulary • extinct	Drawing Conclusions	Facts	Personal Response		
Unit 11		Fiction, Imaginative	Narrator	Vocabulary • frantic	Problem	Action	Inference	Characterization, Written		
Unit 12		Fiction, Imaginative	Main Character	Beginning	Initiating Event	Inference	Middle—Action	End/Drawing Conclusions	Inferring/Fact Personal Response	

Comments: _____

Individual Written Assessment Record (2 of 2)

	Date	Genre Readability	Item 1	Item 2	Item 3	Item 4	Item 5	Item 6	Item 7	Total
Unit 13		Nonfiction	Topic	Note Taking, Facts	Main Idea	Vocabulary • protected	Sequence of Events			
Unit 14		Fiction with Factual Content	Topic	Note Taking, Facts	Vocabulary • mammals	Supporting Details	Vocabulary • carnivores	Sequence of Events		
Unit 15		Nonfiction, Historical	Topic	Goal, Vocabulary • communicate	Supporting Detail	Main Idea	Drawing Conclusions	Inference	Personal Response	
Unit 16		Tall Tale	Characterization	Characterization, Written	Beginning	Drawing Conclusions	Genre • fiction	Genre, Vocabulary • tall tale		
Unit 17		Nonfiction	Main Idea	Supporting Details	Fact Summary, Written	Vocabulary • energy				
Unit 18		Nonfiction	Topic	Supporting Details	Fact Summary, Written	Vocabulary • approximately	Fact			
Unit 19		Fiction, Imaginative	Sequence of Events	Retell, Written	Vocabulary • absurd	Lesson				
Unit 20		Nonfiction	Topic	Supporting Details	Main Idea	Identifying—Fact	Vocabulary • control	Drawing Conclusions, Written		
Unit 21		Nonfiction, Biography	Characterization, Web	Characterization, Written	Vocabulary • inspiring	Cause and Effect	Asking Questions			
Unit 22		Nonfiction, Historical	Vocabulary • inventor	Sequence of Events, Chart	Retell, Written	Vocabulary • creative				
Unit 23		Nonfiction	Supporting Details, Chart, Vocabulary • harsh	Cause and Effect, Chart	Drawing Conclusions	Supporting Details	Main Idea, Inference	Personal Response, Written		
Unit 24		Fiction with Factual Content	Goal, Inference	Setting, Written	Middle—Action	Vocabulary • predator	Cause and Effect, Chart	Idioms and Expressions • green with envy	Asking Questions	

Note: Gray shaded boxes are objectives achieved through inference.

1. SOUND REVIEW Use selected Sound Cards from Units ____–____.

2. SOUNDING OUT SMOOTHLY Have students say the underlined part, sound out and read each word, then read the row.

_____   _____   _____   _____

3. ACCURACY/FLUENCY BUILDING Have students say any underlined part, then read each word. Next, have students read the column.

A1 Sound Practice	**B1** Mixed Practice	**C1** Rhyming Words	**D1**
_____	_____	_____	_____
_____	_____	_____	_____
_____	_____	_____	_____
_____	_____	_____	_____
_____	_____	_____	_____
_____	_____	_____	_____
_____	_____	_____	_____

4. TRICKY WORDS Have students read each row for accuracy, then fluency.

Ⓐ

Ⓑ

5. MULTISYLLABIC WORDS Have students read the word by parts, tell how many syllables are in the word, then read the whole word.

Ⓐ

Ⓑ

Ⓒ

6. DICTATION Say the word. Have students say the word, then say each sound as they touch or write it.

A1	**B1**
_____	_____
_____	_____
_____	_____